MICROWAVE COOKING

FOR YOUR

BABY&CHILD

MICROWAVE COOKING

FOR YOUR

BABY & CHILD

ILLUSTRATIONS BY AGI BEHAN

THE ABCs OF CREATING QUICK,
NUTRITIOUS MEALS FOR LITTLE ONES

EILEEN BEHAN, R.D.

VILLARD BOOKS · NEW YORK · 1991

Grateful acknowledgment is made to the American Academy of Pediatrics for permission to reprint illustrations and descriptions from the Choking/CPR section of the *First Aid Chart*. Copyright © 1989 American Academy of Pediatrics.

Library of Congress Cataloging-in-Publication Data
Behan, Eileen.
    Microwave cooking for your baby and child: the ABCs of creating quick, nutritious meals for little ones/by Eileen Behan.
        p.   cm.
    Includes index.
    ISBN 0-394-58419-8
    1. Cookery (Baby foods).   2. Microwave cookery.   3. Infants—Nutrition.   I. Title.
TX740.B449   1991
641.5′622—dc20   90-50221

Manufactured in the United States of America

9   8   7   6   5   4   3   2

First Edition

DESIGNED BY BARBARA MARKS

To David, Sarah and Emily

my source of

joy and inspiration

THE SENSES

Little eyes see pretty things,
Little noses smell what is sweet,
Little ears hear pleasant sounds,
Mouth likes luscious things to eat.

—Chinese Nursery Rhyme

ACKNOWLEDGMENTS

I once heard it said that writing a cookbook is not a solo effort, and now I know how true that statement is. I had a lot of support and technical advice from many people and I appreciated all of it.

For support, criticism, comments and suggestions I must thank my family, starting with my parents, John and Elizabeth Behan, who always told me to pursue my goals and then gave me the tools to do just that (a very special thanks to Mom, too, for recipe testing). To Sheila, who never failed to ask about "the book," and to Sharon and Kevin, who never doubted I'd accomplish the task. To Kathy, Chuck and Tory, who as a family provided inspiration for parts of this book.

When writing about something medical or scientific, two heads are better than one, and I'd like to thank the following people who reviewed all or part of this manuscript for accuracy or comments: Dr. William Dietz, M.D., Richard E. Mudgett, Ph.D., Marilyn DeSimone, R.D., and Madeline Walsh, R.D.

For artwork I'd like to thank Agi Behan.

Thanks to Trish Cronan and Brad Lavigne, who have been two of my best sources for refining and developing ideas. To Susan Yorstin, and Gale and Kara Day, thank you for comments and recipe testing.

To Judith Paige, a very special thanks for all your contributions.

To Ralph McCue, thank you for your words of encouragement. I only wish you were with us to see the final results.

To Alison Acker, who through her fine editing and skillful suggestions made this a better book, and thank you to Tom Fiffer, Alison's assistant. I am also grateful to the other people at Villard whose contributions were so important: Richard Aquan, Janis Donnaud, Nancy Inglis, Corinne Lewkowicz and Barbara Marks.

To Carol Mann, thanks for seeing the potential in my idea.

CONTENTS

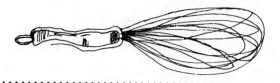

INTRODUCTION:
THE MICROWAVE SOLUTION

If a magic genie appeared to new parents and allowed them to create the ideal cooking system for babies and small children, I'm sure they'd come up with something fast and nutritious that involved little cleanup. *Voilà*, the microwave!

My husband, David, and I purchased our first microwave about six months before the birth of our daughter Sarah. We never felt the need for "instant" cooking, but with the impending change a baby would bring we thought we'd take advantage of every modern convenience. In truth we hardly used it until Sarah started to eat. Boiling a cup of water and defrosting were what I thought a microwave oven did best. I suspect I was like most cooks who just never took the time to master it.

Mothers and fathers today have many choices and decisions to make about feeding their babies. You can buy commercially prepared jars of ready-to-eat food or cans of dehydrated baby food that just need reconstituting. You can also take foods from the family table and simply purée them, or you can cook your baby's food fresh from scratch. So how do you choose?

Your personal situation will determine how and what you feed your baby. You've probably already asked your pediatrician about safe feeding practices, probably read a few magazine articles on the subject, then balanced the time you have for cooking against the time you have for your husband, other children and family members, community commitments and work responsibilities. After taking into account all these considerations, you make decisions about how to feed your baby that will work for you and your family.

In many cases you've probably chosen a combination of feeding possibilities. If you're traveling and don't have a kitchen, then a jar of ready-to-eat food for your baby may work best. When the family is eating a simple meal of chicken, potatoes, and vegetables, then a quick purée in the blender works nicely. When take-out pizza is on the adult menu, making baby a meal all his own may be the solution that day. But for cooking healthy food that babies and children love, nothing beats the microwave.

When babies grow into toddlers, they can share much of what you're serving on the adult table, and your microwave may become the primary cooking tool for all of you, or you may still just use it to prepare your child's meals. The same qualities that make a microwave ideal for cooking small babies' meals still apply to older children, and many mothers simply adapt their recipes to suit their child's tastes. In this book I've included recipes for children from tiny babies all the way through age three, but if your children are like mine, they'll keep asking for their favorite "baby" foods even beyond that age. And why not? The recipes are good for your preschooler or school-age child for the same reasons they're good for your toddler. They're low in salt, offer a lot of variety and, most of all, the recipes in Chapters 9 and 10 provide a balanced meal in one dish.

...

When my daughter started on solid foods, I was dissatisfied with the choices offered on supermarket shelves. I wanted her to have fresh-cooked foods and more variety. Besides being a parent like you, I am also a professional nutritionist. I counsel adults, mothers-to-be, even children and teenagers, about nutrition and diet. I feel strongly that good, healthy food served to children when they're young helps lay the foundation for good health and eating habits when they're grown up. So when cooking for Sarah, I did what I thought a mother was supposed to do: I steamed the vegetables and boiled the potato, baked the chicken, then ground or mashed it all up into a consistency Sarah could handle: nice, soft mush. At the end of one meal I'd have three or four dirty pans, not including the utensils or dishes she used, and I still had to cook dinner for the grown-ups. Finally, I got smart and decided to tap the resources of my microwave.

MICROWAVE COOKING AND NUTRITION

Microwave cooking is ideally suited for making your baby and child delicious meals and snacks. Cooking fast, which is what your microwave does best, retains more nutrients than slow cooking or boiling methods. A microwave cooks with little or no added liquid, and that means that no nutrients are lost or discarded in the cooking water. It also cooks fast, so nutrients are less likely to be destroyed. In fact, studies show that microwave cooking retains more vitamin C and more B vitamins—thiamine, riboflavin, pyridoxine and folic acid—than conventional cooking methods. The microwave oven also retains more flavor and color—particularly of vegetables—and this increases the chance that baby will want to eat them.

The microwave works quickly (particularly on baby-size portions), which in itself should be enough to convince you to convert to using one, and since microwave ovens cook by moist heat, the foods you cook in them will come out tender and wet, qualities that grown-ups might dislike but kids love. Remember, no matter how wholesome a dinner might be on paper, it isn't nutritious if your baby doesn't eat it! In the early feeding stages, when baby needs her food puréed, it is easier to do it if the foods are still juicy after cooking.

Baby stews and one-dish minicasseroles are ideally suited for baby—and for busy mothers (and fathers) who want to avoid elaborate cleanups. Since microwave cooking times are short, food doesn't get cooked onto the dishware. The same dish can go from freezer to oven to table, making cleanup so quick you'll hardly notice it.

The microwave has a whole host of other advantages: In the heat of summer, when you may be satisfied with just a salad, you'll still have to make dinner for your little ones. With your microwave oven you can cook without heating up the kitchen. And when fruit such as green bananas or hard pears aren't soft enough for baby, you can "ripen" them quickly in the microwave.

So, if all you've been using your microwave oven for is making tea, reheating leftovers and cooking TV dinners, you're about to be introduced to a whole new horizon of cooking possibilities.

SAFETY FIRST

Despite the fact that more than three-fourths of American homes now have microwave ovens, you still may have a nagging concern about safety. "Does using the microwave mean I'm nuking my baby's food?" is a question I've been asked by more than one parent. Rest assured: There's a world of difference between nuclear radiation and the energy produced by your microwave. The waves in your oven are similar to radio waves, and once food is cooked they simply dissipate. They *don't* stay in food, and baby *doesn't* eat them.

The real safety issues when preparing baby food (whether using a microwave or a conventional oven) are preventing burns from food that is too hot and food poisoning from food that is undercooked. All the recipes and cooking methods I use are healthy, and microwave safety is simple. Be sure, though, to read the sections on safety. They explain why I recommend preparing foods in a certain way and help you use the microwave with complete confidence.

Microwave ovens are so safe and easy to use that many parents feel safe letting their children cook their own meals. After all, a parent reasons, if a child can learn to press the right buttons, using the microwave is so much safer than lighting the oven or using the stove top. This is true, but I think it makes parents *over*confident. No small child should *ever* be left to use any cooking utensil —microwaves included—unsupervised.

Though the recipes in this book can be served to kids of all ages, *not* all children should be using the microwave oven. When surveyed, many parents stated that they felt the microwave oven was safer for their child to use than a conventional oven. The logic here is that the conventional oven gets hot while the microwave only heats the food, and therefore they assume that risk of burns is less with the microwave. That is not true, and in fact many young children have been scalded and burned while removing or eating food prepared in the microwave. Most children don't understand the potential troubles associated with uneven cooking. While some areas of a cooked dish may be

scalding hot, another part may be undercooked and carrying bacteria that could cause illness.

There is disagreement about what age a child can safely use the microwave. Some say seven is old enough; others say wait until your child is twelve. One guideline that seems reasonable to me is to wait until your child is capable of reading well and can easily see into the oven without standing on a stool or a chair. A child who cannot read the oven's operating instructions or the cooking instructions on a frozen-food package should not be operating the microwave oven, and a child who isn't tall enough to see into the oven is in danger of spilling hot food and getting a nasty burn.

A MICROWAVE COOKBOOK

Obviously, there's more to feeding your baby than learning how to use the microwave. When I was faced with feeding my first daughter for the first time, I can honestly say that I was worried. Even though I'm a dietitian, my experience with kids and food was mostly out of a textbook. I was the youngest in my family, too, so I never had much experience feeding babies.

When it came down to just me and Sarah in the kitchen, I had the same concerns all new mothers have. I wondered how much to feed and how often. I speculated about the health benefits and disadvantages of serving whole grains, beans, fish, even the so-called gassy vegetables. I looked through my nutrition books and found specific feeding advice sparse.

So, to help other mothers and myself, I read just about everything relating to food that was put out by the American Academy of Pediatrics in the last ten years and culled the medical journals and pediatric textbooks to find answers to my specific questions. The results of my research can be found in this book.

In Part 1 you'll find a month-by-month feeding schedule, information about preventing allergies and when to introduce a variety of foods safely. Health concerns such as obesity and cholesterol are common dinner-table conversation these days, so you'll find clear information on these health issues to help guide your feeding decisions.

In Part 2 you'll get some hands-on advice about how and what to cook. Plain foods are on baby's first-foods list. I've included an index of the top one hundred most-asked-about foods. Most are foods I think should be on every baby's menu, either because they taste good or because they are very nutritious. Along with cooking suggestions are nutrition and storage tips.

Also included are foods that don't need cooking, such as cheese and crackers. Some surprises, such as sugar and bacon, are in the index, too. I don't recommend these as baby foods, but I think parents need to know how and if these items can fit into a child's menu.

Part 3 will provide you with more than fifty easy and satisfying recipes for complete one-dish meals, divided into four age groups from infants through three-year-olds. I've included a chapter on healthy breakfast ideas, and one with yummy suggestions for desserts, too. There is also an important section on what to feed your child when he is sick, and a question-and-answer section that contains the problems and concerns parents ask me about most.

In writing *Microwave Cooking for Your Baby and Child* I hoped to create a feeding resource for parents of young children. It was my intention to provide enough information in a clear manner to help parents be confident about feeding their babies and to help them raise happy, healthy kids—and have fun doing it. I hope I have been successful.

MICROWAVE
COOKING
FOR YOUR
BABY&CHILD

PART
1

GETTING

STARTED

1

SAFETY FIRST

If you've cooked with a microwave, you've already discovered that the heat can be uneven. You take your dinner out of the oven only to find half of it red-hot and the other half still cold or barely warm. For you this may be slightly annoying, but for babies it poses a serious risk. Uneven heating can cause "hot spots" to form—areas of food that get very hot while others remain cool to the touch. If you feed your child a lump of food that is cool on the surface but hot in the middle, her mouth—which is much more sensitive to temperature than yours is—can get burned. To avoid burning your baby's mouth on these hot spots, always stir food to distribute the heat and check it by trying a bite yourself before serving. Then, to make doubly sure, give it what I

call the "clean-finger poke test." Using a clean finger, poke the food in a couple of places just to make sure it's cool enough to eat. This might sound odd, but there is *nothing* wrong with sticking a clean finger into your baby's meal, particularly if it will protect her from a harmful burn.

Here's one safety rule that may come as a surprise: The microwave is ideal for making baby food, but it should *not* be used to heat formula. Emergency rooms across the country have reported nasty mouth burns from babies who've been served bottles heated in the microwave. What happens is, you put the bottle in the microwave to take the chill off, maybe for a minute. When you take it out, it feels warm to the touch— perfect for baby. But below that surface of warm milk is milk that is scalding hot, causing your baby to burn her mouth as soon as she starts drinking. Now, I know there are those of you who will read this and say, "Oh, Eileen is overreacting. I heat the bottle in the microwave, shake it before serving and have never burned my baby." Well, you're right. I know mothers who have warmed bottles in the microwave and carefully checked them before serving. I'm not going to recommend this practice, though, because the possibility of burning your baby *does* exist. If you do insist on warming bottles in the microwave, *please be extremely careful.* There's no safe way to gauge accurately the temperature of liquids in a bottle. By not recommending this I hope to make mothers and baby-sitters keep their guard up. I warm bottles the way our parents did —by either running the bottle under warm tap water or letting it sit in a bath of hot water until it tests warm—and I make sure my sitters know not to heat bottles in the microwave.

Cooking safely with a microwave starts at the supermarket. Once you've passed through the checkout line, get perishable food items home as quickly as possible and refrigerate or freeze those that need it. When preparing food, always use clean cooking utensils. Be especially careful to clean cutting boards and knives after cutting meat, fish or poultry, because improper cleaning can cross-contaminate food. For example, a knife used to cut raw poultry could contain harmful bacteria. If you then use that same knife to cut an apple, your baby could ingest those bacteria when he eats the apple slices.

Also, always keep vegetables and fruits cold, because they start to lose nutrition at warmer temperatures. And be sure to use dairy products such as cheese, yogurt and milk before the expiration date on the label. Finally, whenever a food seems the slightest bit spoiled, has an off odor, or is oozing, leaking or bulging inside the package or can, *throw it out.* Don't even bother to taste it, because making your baby sick is *not* worth the small amount of money you might save. Because your baby's ability to fight off food contaminants is not as strong as yours is, you should never serve him any raw animal-protein foods. That includes raw beef and seafood such as sushi or shellfish. As an extra precaution, don't serve raw or cooked shellfish such as shrimp, clams, mussels and oysters if they still contain the intestinal tract. These foods when eaten whole may contain some bacteria that can't be disarmed by your baby's immune system.

There has been concern that food poisoning can result from cooking foods such as meat, poultry or fish in the microwave. Rest assured, the microwave *can and does* cook food to temperatures high enough to kill bacteria. However, if food is not uniformly heated, some areas that contain bacteria may not get hot enough to kill potentially harmful organisms. Here's how to prevent problems:

1. Cook meat, fish and poultry until steaming hot.
2. Rotate or stir foods while cooking to distribute the heat.
3. Cover foods during or after cooking to keep heat in and allow for even heat distribution.

HOW LONG FOODS WILL KEEP

The following is a storage guideline for keeping foods wholesome at home.

Milk:	Use within five days of the "sell by" date.
Eggs:	Keep no longer than 4 to 5 weeks in the refrigerator in their original container.
Poultry:	1 to 2 days in the fridge fresh or cooked; 6 months frozen.
Meat:	Beef, veal, lamb, pork, roasts, steaks, ribs: 3 to 4 days in the refrigerator; 3 to 6 months in the freezer.
Fish:	Use fresh fish within a few hours. Cooked fish will keep 3 to 4 days, and when frozen will last 3 to 6 months.
Vegetables:	Use root vegetables such as potatoes, carrots and parsnips in 7 to 14 days. Use broccoli, cauliflower and Brussels sprouts in 3 to 5 days. Use leafy or soft vegetables such as spinach or tomatoes within 3 to 4 days.

4. Allow foods to "rest," covered, before serving. Resting simply allows the food to sit, still covered, for at least 2 to 5 minutes after you have removed it from the oven. This will kill any lingering microbes.
5. Another way to make sure meat is fully cooked is to check the temperature. If

you don't already have a food thermometer, buy one at your local hardware or kitchen store. Cook beef to 160°; cook veal, pork and lamb to 170°; and cook poultry to 185°.

6. When defrosting, use meats right away— don't allow them to sit at room temperature. And when reheating, get foods really hot, not just lukewarm.

In some cases, the microwave has actually been credited with *preventing* food poisoning. In Tennessee, thirteen workers at the same mill all ate hamburgers from the same fast-food restaurant, but only one came down with hepatitis. Health officials discovered that the one sick worker had eaten her burger fresh from the restaurant, while the other twelve reheated theirs in a microwave back at the plant. The hepatitis A virus, which was attached to the hamburger buns, was effectively deactivated by reheating in the microwave. Score one safety point for the mike!

Although I mentioned this in the introduction, it is important enough to say again. Parents must be cautious when letting any child use the microwave oven. I think a good safety rule is that a child who can't read well and can't see into the oven without standing on a stool should not be allowed to use a microwave alone. A microwave seems easy to use, but a burn is a serious injury and it's simply not worth taking any risks. If you have to be away from home at dinner and are leaving school-age children alone, my advice is to provide foods they can eat cold.

THE RIGHT STUFF

I don't believe in buying a lot of unnecessary gadgets when you have a baby. But some things, like high chairs, you just can't do without. Based on my experience, here are some pointers for choosing useful feeding equipment, including my research on microwave ovens.

If you have a child or children and have somehow escaped buying or being given a microwave, you should shop carefully when you decide to get one. First, buy the oven with the most power and space that you can afford, preferably a 650- or 700-watt machine with at least a 1.5-cubic-foot capacity—large and powerful enough to cook a whole turkey. You won't need all that space to cook for baby, but once you master your microwave, you'll want it to cook whole meals for your family.

Buying a powerful oven is essential. My first oven was only 500 watts, and it took twenty minutes to bake a potato. When I bought a 700-watt oven I was amazed at the difference in cooking times. Now I can have a delicious baked potato in five minutes, and I'll never return to a slower oven.

As far as options are concerned, don't spend your money on temperature probes, special computer timing or fancy cooking mechanisms. I have found no use for these items, and the consensus among food writers I've read seems to be the same: You don't need them and they inflate the price.

The one gadget worth investing in, however, is an automatic carousel that turns the food as it cooks. This helps to ensure even cooking. If your oven does not come with a carousel, you can buy one at your favorite kitchen shop.

I would bet that if I asked those of you who own microwaves, you couldn't tell me how much wattage your oven has or how big it is. You're not alone. A recent informal survey in the *Boston Globe* found that only one out of nine owners could correctly report their oven's size. Of course, as they say, size isn't everything, but if you want recipes to turn out right, you must know how big— and how powerful—your oven is. Here's a quick and easy test: Fill a microwave-safe dish with one cup of cool tap water. Place it in the oven and cook it at full power until it boils. If it boils in under three minutes, you have a 600- to 700-watt oven. If it takes more than three minutes, your oven is in the 500- to 600-watt range. And for those of you who saved it, there's always your owner's manual for reference.

A NOTE ON THE RECIPES

The recipes in this book are all "user-friendly." If you follow the cooking times, you'll never ruin a dish by overcooking. But since I tested all the recipes in a full-size oven, you may need to increase cooking times if your oven is smaller and less powerful. See Chapter 5 for a chart on adjusting recipes to match oven capacity.

HOW THE MICROWAVE WORKS

Your microwave oven works by producing "short" waves of energy, called microwaves, which are similar to radio waves. These waves bounce around in the oven until the food absorbs them. Once absorbed they cause the water and salt molecules in the food to rotate, and these fast-moving molecules create heat and cook the food.

Because the microwaves actually penetrate only about a half inch deep, smaller baby-size portions cook quite fast. Large items—like roasts—cook more slowly, as the heat is conducted into the deeper layers of the meat. Since most foods for toddlers are prepared in small portions, the microwave is virtually the best place to cook for your baby.

SELECTING UTENSILS FOR THE MICROWAVE OVEN

Your kitchen is probably already equipped with dishes that will work in the microwave and for feeding baby. Glass and ceramic dishes work especially well, and any serving dish, plate, jar or cup that is heat-tolerant can be used. But *don't ever* use any metal pans, saucepans or containers in the microwave. They can block microwaves, prevent cooking and damage the oven. Even dishes with decorative metal trims and decorative paints are not suitable for microwave cooking. There are a number of utensils now being marketed for the microwave. Look for a dish that is labeled "microwave safe." I personally prefer clear glass cookware with lids that fit well.

Always choose a dish that is the right size for the recipe and for the amount being served to your baby. (For the recipes in this book, 2- to 4-cup capacity will work nicely.) And since you'll often be serving your baby's meal in the same bowl you cooked it in, try to choose one that is pretty, too. Baby may be too small to notice, but *you* may as well pick something appealing. Remember, too, that not all dishes are made for microwave use. To test a dish for safety, try this method: Place the dish, along with a glass of water, in your microwave for one minute. If the water gets hot and the dish doesn't, it's safe to use. But if the dish gets hot, it is absorbing microwaves, which will slow cooking times, weaken the structure and eventually damage the dish. Don't use margarine tubs, yogurt or reusable plastic containers for cooking or reheating in the microwave. The heat from the food can actually melt the container and start a fire. Use only plastic cookware labeled "microwave safe."

Most foods should be covered when cooking. This keeps hot steam trapped, speeds cooking, and makes for more even cooking. Instead of using plastic wrap, I recommend you use a glass lid or perhaps a dinner plate as a cover. Plastic wrap does make a tighter cover and may keep food moister, but there is the danger that when heated the plastic wrap may release harmful chemicals that can migrate onto the food. So don't use plastic wrap as a cover. Glass is the perfect medium, because when heated it releases no harmful chemicals. Always be careful when you remove covers, as hot steam builds up and can cause a nasty burn to the cook. I recommend using insulated gloves or pads when handling foods in the microwave oven. Even though the oven does not heat the dish, the food, once hot, can.

Since we are on the subject of plastics and containers, let me mention a concern that you're certain to hear more about. To meet the demand by consumers for crisp, browned food like waffles, pizza, and fish sticks, frozen food companies have inserted metallic strips and discs into their cooking packages. These materials get so hot that they cause the food to brown. The problem is that these packaging materials have been tested for safety only at temperatures that reach 300 degrees, and now they are being used in the microwave and getting as hot as 500 degrees. At these very high levels, potential cancer-causing substances may be released and enter the food that you and your family eats. No one knows for sure how dangerous these packages might be. The Food and Drug Administration will be issuing guidelines when it completes its investigation. For now, I would definitely avoid the frozen microwavable foods that use this type of packaging.

THE FEEDING SETUP

No matter how delicious your microwave meals are, baby won't eat if she's not seated comfortably. It is now recommended that most babies start on solids at four to six months. In these early months, before sitting in an upright position becomes commonplace, the chair or seat you choose for feeding is crucial. It should provide your baby with a safe, secure place to eat and should allow you to have free hands and easy access to baby.

Before graduating to a real high chair, many mothers start with an infant seat. These can be fine, as long as you choose one that can be placed in a near-upright position and has good, secure safety straps. You don't want to feed baby while she's lying down.

As your child reaches six months, weighs more, and is more active, the infant chair may not be stable enough. If, like most parents, you put the chair on the table or counter, to bring baby to a comfortable feeding height, a busy, restless baby may be at risk of falling off. So be careful!

When you finally do buy a high chair, you'll have it for a long time, so choose wisely. Your chair should:
- Be sturdy (not wobbly);
- Have legs spaced far enough apart to prevent tipping;

- Have a tray that slides on and off and fits tightly when in place. A tray that can be removed with one hand is helpful, too—you'll always have something in your other hand, either food, baby or bottle;
- Have a strong safety strap that goes between the legs and around the waist;
- Be attractive, because it will be in your kitchen for a long time.

If the chair is wooden, you'll need a pad for the seat, particularly for the head. The pad should attach securely, allowing for minimal slipping. Also, try to find a chair that can be pulled close to the table when baby no longer needs a tray. Finally, avoid a chair that has intricate detailing. This will catch baby food, which, when dried, has the unique property of turning into a hard-to-clean substance much like cement.

CAUTION

Never leave baby alone in a high chair, and don't expect the tray alone to keep him in his chair. Always use the safety strap!

OTHER ESSENTIALS

- Bibs: Personally, I don't like the cute little cloth bibs. They worked fine when my girls just drank milk, but when solids became part of the menu, we needed more protection. I prefer the stiff, heavy plastic bibs that can be wiped clean. Choose one that has a pocket at the bottom—it will catch the food and drink that doesn't make it into baby's mouth.
- Spoons: It's definitely worthwhile to buy a baby spoon, because regular family spoons are much too big for first-time eaters. You should also have at least two spoons, because by age nine months your baby will want to hold one while you use the other to make sure at least some of the food reaches its destination.
- Cups: At around eight months you can try offering baby liquids in a cup. Cups with lids can be very helpful. For young drinkers select a small, narrow one that has a lidded spout with only one hole in it. The absence of a second air hole means that liquid will flow out of the cup more slowly. For older children, try a cup with handles and with several holes in the lid.
- Plates: *Always use nonbreakable serving dishes for children.* Plastic dishes with suction cups on the bottom are handy when children start to experiment with falling

and flying objects. And remember that even though the microwave itself doesn't make plates hot, the heat from the food *can* be transferred to the plate, making it hot to the touch. To prevent problems, transfer the food to another dish or simply wait until it cools before serving. Not all plates and dishes are microwave-safe. You can either buy dishes made especially for use in the microwave or, as a rule of thumb, test a dish for safety by placing the dish, along with a glass of water, in your oven. Cook at full power for one minute. If the glass of water gets hot and not the empty dish, it's safe.

3

RIGHT FROM THE START

 Thank goodness that as new parents we're not plunged into complex feeding decisions right from birth! The only choice to be made on day one is whether to breast- or bottle-feed, and most of us, even when bleary-eyed from lack of sleep, can manage either. Not until months later do we start our babies on solid foods, and by that stage we've mastered diapering, bathing and the art of getting more than three hours of sleep. What better time for a new challenge: learning to cook with your microwave!

FIRST THINGS FIRST

In the beginning, formula, breast milk or a combination of the two are all your little one needs. The only question is, How much? Truth to tell, there are no strict limits. A breast-fed baby should probably be offered the breast on demand five to ten times a day, and formula-fed newborn babies can drink anywhere from sixteen to thirty-two ounces. But every baby is different. A good rule to follow in those first weeks of life is simply to feed your baby on demand. When your baby cries for food—*feed him.* Some babies need to eat every two hours and all through the night. Other infants can sleep for long stretches without getting hungry. Don't worry about "spoiling" your child at this young age: Feeding him when he cries for food is likely to make him more secure and trustful, not spoiled. Little babies cry because they need you, not because they're trying to be manipulative. If you're worried about your baby's feeding schedule, get on the phone to your pediatrician. Most doctors are happy to answer feeding questions, as are the nurses they work with. In the first two weeks at home with my daughter, I was on the phone five times to my pediatrician's office asking all kinds of nervous new-mom questions—and Sarah wasn't even sick!

In many cases you can call the hospital where you delivered your baby and ask the nurses in the nursery for feeding advice, too.

WHEN TO START SOLIDS

If you are a first-time parent, you're probably especially anxious to introduce your baby to whole foods. It is best, however, if you wait until baby is at least four months old. At four to six months, most babies can learn to swallow more than just liquids. Simultaneously, their digestive tracts mature and they can digest foods other than breast milk and formula. Until now your baby got all her nutrition from her milk, but at six months she needs more iron and vitamin C than milk alone can provide. Two excellent sources of these nutrients are iron-fortified cereal and vitamin C–rich fruit or juice.

Equally important as baby's improved ability to digest and swallow is her newfound ability to communicate. At six months a baby can show hunger by opening her mouth and leaning forward or disinterest by turning away and leaning back. If your child hates a particular food, you'll soon know it. If baby didn't have these communication skills you might unintentionally force-feed your child. Feeding should be a pleasant experience for both parent and baby, so pay attention to what baby tells you.

One question many new parents ask is, Do breast-fed babies need food sooner? Most pediatricians continue to advice that solid food be delayed until at least four months. There have been several recent studies, though, that suggest that breast-fed babies may need food sooner. One study of thirty-three infants fed breast milk exclusively for the first six months found that the infants went from the sixty-seventh percentile for weight down to the forty-seventh percentile in that time. In a Finnish study, growth in exclusively breast-fed infants slowed after only three months.

Does this mean that if you're breast-feeding you must introduce foods sooner? Not at all. Each time your child is weighed at the two-, four- and six-month checkups, the doctor will track your child's weight progress. If there is any significant change or undesirable pattern in weight or height, your pediatrician can and should give you personalized feeding advice. If growth seems to falter, your pediatrician may advise the introduction of solid foods sooner. As for vitamin supplements, follow the advice of your baby's doctor, *if* he or she advises them. Doctors routinely recommend supplements of vitamin D for breast-fed babies. Don't forget, however, that breast milk is a high-calorie and very nourishing food, capable of meeting the needs of all healthy babies.

There is no rigid order for introducing solid foods to your baby. I like cereal as a first food because of its convenience and nutritional value, but many babies start off with applesauce or bananas and, of course, are none the worse for it. On the next page is a simple, flexible schedule for introducing and serving foods all the way up to age three. These are, of course, only suggestions. It is also important to remember the five-day rule: Always allow five days before introducing a new food so that an allergy or food reaction can be detected if present. At this early age it is common for babies to have a food reaction that might manifest itself as a skin rash or just unexplained fussiness. Don't be alarmed. This is almost always a temporary problem. (See Chapter 4 for more information on food allergies.)

At 4 to 6 months you can feed baby:
breast milk
formula
infant cereal—rice, barley, oatmeal
fruit juices—apple, pear

At 6 to 8 months you can add:
juices—apricot, cranberry
strained or mashed vegetables without
    skins, peels or seeds
fresh, ripe or cooked fruit without skins,
    peels or seeds
teething biscuits
plain yogurt

At 8 to 12 months you can add:
cow's milk
cereal—all varieties, including corn and
    wheat, but *not* cereal with added sugar
    and dried fruit or nuts because both are
    easy for baby to choke on (see Chapter
    4 for more information about choking)
grains—white and brown rice, cornmeal,
    buckwheat, millet, barley
pasta and noodles
finger foods—toast, crackers, bread, bagels
juice—all varieties, including tomato and
    orange
fruits—all, served mashed or cut up
vegetables—all mashed or cut up
protein foods—lean meat, chicken, fish,

egg yolks, yogurt, peanut butter,
beans, prepared to a consistency your
baby can swallow

At 12 to 36 months a child can eat almost
anything you do. But foods must still be
served in an easily chewable (or
gummable, if the child is under 2)
form. Also, avoid those items that go
to taste extremes, such as spicy or salty
foods.

STRATEGIES FOR A SUCCESSFUL FIRST MEAL

When introducing real food to baby, pick a
time when she's not ravenously hungry. A
baby crying out for her usual milk feeding
isn't going to be happy with some lumpy goo
that you shove into her mouth. She'll just
get frustrated and cry louder. Give her some
breast milk or formula first to calm her
down, *then* offer her the cereal. Make sure
she's comfortable, in an upright position.
Hold her securely on your lap, or use an
infant seat or the high chair. Feed her with
a spoon that fits the shape of her small
mouth, such as a plain or plastic-covered
baby spoon, and offer only a *small* first feeding. And *always use a spoon! Never mix and
feed solids from a bottle,* unless you want your

baby to learn how to drink food instead of eat it.

So, you've done all this, followed the instructions, and baby still isn't happy. Don't be disappointed if she doesn't greet her first meal enthusiastically. At this point in your baby's feeding development, all you're doing is teaching her to eat. The formula or breast milk you're feeding her still meets most of her nutritional needs. The first time I fed my youngest daughter, she looked at me with disgust, as if I were trying to poison instead of nourish her! Don't be discouraged, take your time and please, remember to *smile*. Eating should be pleasurable—for you *and* your child.

SPECIFIC FOODS AND BEVERAGES
....

BABY'S FIRST FOOD: CEREAL

Why is it that doctors, nutritionists, even grandparents routinely recommend rice as baby's first food? The answer is simple: Rice is unlikely to cause a food allergy or reaction, it's fortified (in the form of infant cereal) with iron, and it's easy to serve in small portions in a form that parallels baby's swallowing abilities.

After rice cereal you can move on to

MIXING CEREAL

Mix 4 tablespoons cereal in a microwave-proof bowl with ¼ to ½ cup room-temperature or cold liquid. Place in the microwave and heat at medium power for 15 to 30 seconds. Stir cereal to eliminate hot spots and taste test it before giving it to baby—just to be sure it's not too hot.

Gradually thicken the consistency by adding more cereal. The liquid used for mixing should be one baby has been drinking. Do not use cow's milk until baby is at least six months old.

---

oatmeal or barley. Both can be bought as infant cereals fortified with iron.

JUICING IT UP

You can offer baby fruit juice at about the same time you start cereal—four to six months. Juice has two purposes: It quenches thirst and should provide vitamin C. Obviously all juice can quench thirst, but not all are rich in vitamin C. Selecting a nutritious juice for your baby isn't always simple because even a juice that claims to be 100 percent fruit juice may contain only 25 or 50 percent of the RDA (Recommended Daily Allowance) for vitamin C.

To make sure your baby gets enough vitamin C, serve fortified infant juices such as grape, apple or pear. When baby is older—after eight or nine months—you can replace the more expensive infant juices with adult varieties of orange juice or grapefruit juice, which are naturally rich in vitamin C. A word of caution, though: Citrus juices served before eight months can cause an allergic reaction.

Be especially wary of fruit blends and juice drinks, and always read labels. If water is the first ingredient followed by sugar or high fructose corn syrup, you're buying flavored sugar water and not real juice. Fruit blends may be 100 percent fruit juice, but the juice may not contain much vitamin C. They may also contain added sugar in the form of high fructose corn syrup. And some juice products, meant for older children, contain only part juice and are mostly flavored sugar water.

Once you've chosen the best juice, be cautious about how much baby drinks, particularly in the second year of life. Too much can cause diarrhea and diminish the child's appetite for other, nutritious foods. My daughter Emily always liked juice, but after her first birthday she started liking it too much. Juice seemed to kill her appetite for meals. The solution I came up with was to offer her one full glass of vitamin C–rich juice at breakfast and one or two whole fruits during the day. The juice and fruit satisfied her nutritional needs. Then, to quench her thirst, I gave her a glass with one part juice and three parts water. She didn't mind the diluted drink at all, and I didn't mind her drinking it since it didn't have enough calories to ruin her appetite.

VITAMIN C IN JUICE

The vitamin C content for the following juices is for an 8-ounce serving (a baby needs 30 to 40 milligrams per day):

apple	2 milligrams
cranberry juice cocktail	40 milligrams
grape	trace
grapefruit	99 milligrams
orange	120 milligrams
pineapple	23 milligrams
tomato	39 milligrams

Source: USDA Handbook 456. None of the juices listed are fortified with vitamin C. Apple and grape juice can be purchased with vitamin C added.

COW'S MILK

Postpone serving your baby cow's milk until he is at least six months old. This recommendation comes from the American Academy of Pediatrics, and for several good reasons. In simplest terms, cow's milk is designed for baby calves, not your baby boy or girl. Feeding your baby cow's milk before age six months can aggravate an allergy or contribute to iron-deficiency anemia. Cow's milk is hard for very young babies to digest. It can cause minute amounts of blood loss in the digestive tract that could lead to anemia. In addition, cow's milk is extremely low in both iron and vitamin C, which helps in the absorption of iron. So baby should not drink cow's milk unless he is old enough to have a more developed digestive system and is getting enough solid foods to provide an adequate intake of iron and vitamin C.

Once cow's milk does replace breast milk or formula, baby's intake of solid foods should increase to provide at least half the calories needed for a day. Feeding your baby more than one quart per day is not advised, because at this level baby will get too many calories from milk and won't be able to eat enough solid foods to provide a balanced diet.

Even though cow's milk can be started safely at six months, most pediatricians and

ALAR AND INFANT APPLE JUICE— WHAT YOU NEED TO KNOW NOW!

Many parents are concerned about the presence in apple juice of the chemical Alar, which has been discovered to pose a cancer risk. In an independent study of infant apple juices conducted in 1989 Consumers Union found infant apple juice distributed by Beech-Nut and Gerber to have undetectable levels of Alar. Heinz products had an Alar level well below the levels found in adult apple-juice products. Before the Alar scare, many babies were drinking adult apple juice and not the *Alar-free* infant juices. Alar is no longer being applied to our apple crops, but some Alar-treated apples may still be in storage. Until there is no more Alar in adult apple-juice products, you should feed your baby only the varieties of apple juice that are marketed for infants, not adults. These infant juices are apparently scrutinized for Alar contamination more carefully by manufacturers.

There's no need to feel that apple juice must be part of your baby's diet, either. Apples may cause fewer food reactions at an early age, but apple juice is no more nutritious than other fortified juices. I've always thought that apple juice is so popular because it doesn't stain clothes the way darker juices can—and every mother and dad has laundry to think about, too.

WHOLE VERSUS SKIM MILK

As adults we are all weight-conscious, but babyhood is *not* the time to start calorie counting. *Always give baby whole milk, not low-fat or skim.* Your baby *must* have the fat that whole milk provides to ensure proper brain development.

nutritionists would rather see children continue on formula or breast milk until their first birthday. Most of us start baby on cow's milk simply because it's cheaper than formula and more convenient. To save some money, give a combination of both milk and formula. For instance, after six months, try using cow's milk to mix with cereal or other foods, but still use formula for feeding.

WATER

In the first four to six months, healthy babies do not require any extra water—they get enough fluid from breast milk or formula. Extra fluids are needed only during illnesses such as diarrhea and vomiting, or if outside temperatures are extremely high. Check with your pediatrician if you are worried about any of these conditions. When you start your baby on solid foods, you'll want to offer water, because water helps with diges-

tion. But don't overdo it by letting baby fill up on water. Babies have small stomachs, and offering water right before a meal might fill him up and keep him from eating. Instead, offer water with food at mealtimes in either a bottle or a cup.

Lead

If you drink from your own well and have noticed a change in the color or taste of the water or suspect your pipes may contain lead, you may want to have your water tested for safety. Call the Environmental Protection Agency (1-800-426-4791) for a list of certified water testers in your area.

Water that travels through lead-lined pipes can carry traces of this poison and cause serious impairments. A recent EPA survey found that 42 million Americans were drinking water that had a lead content in excess of the proposed safe limit of 20 parts per billion. If your pipes are a dull gray instead of shiny, or if the plumbing in your house is more than eighty years old, you may have lead in your water. If you suspect that you have lead-containing water pipes, have the water tested. You can reduce your risk of consuming lead in drinking water by doing the following: Use cold water and not hot tap water, because hot water can dissolve lead. *Use cold tap water, then heat it.* Let the water run for a few minutes before using it, too. Water left standing overnight can pick up lead. For a free pamphlet, "Lead in Your Drinking Water," see the appendix.

Pollution

To avoid pollution, many people have turned to bottled drinking water. But bottled water may not be the answer. By law, bottled water does not need to be any cleaner than the water already coming out of your tap. In fact, some bottled water actually *is* tap water. And while community water supplies are routinely tested for safety, there is no similar monitoring program for bottled water. If you use bottled water, call your supplier and ask for a copy of its water-test results, then compare this with the standards put out by the EPA (see above for the toll-free number).

A water-filter system may also appeal to you, but again, be cautious. Unless it is installed and maintained carefully and designed to filter out the contaminants that need to be removed, you may be paying a lot for nothing. For information about water-filter systems, see the appendix.

THE PLOT THICKENS

When your baby has moved on to foods thicker than cereal, you can start introduc-

---

TO BOIL OR NOT TO BOIL

Years ago, our parents had to worry about harmful bacteria in water, so they boiled it before feeding it to us as infants. Now most public water supplies are free from bacterial contamination, but there are other, more complex concerns. Insecticides, high sodium levels and hazardous chemicals have all been found in our drinking water, and simply boiling won't remove them.

---

ing things like mashed banana, applesauce, other strained fruit and mashed vegetables. Stay away, however, from hard-to-digest items such as corn, and fruits or vegetables with peels or skin, and serve only single-ingredient items. Try applesauce, not apple cobbler; plain mashed banana, not banana yogurt. Also, the foods you serve your baby in the fourth through eighth months must match his swallowing ability. First foods should be smooth, the consistency of applesauce or yogurt. Consult My Top One Hundred (see page 65) to find out how to prepare a variety of foods to match your baby's age.

At about the eighth month, baby discovers how to use his fingers and can now try soft table and finger foods, such as toast or sliced peeled fruits. Baby is now old enough to try protein-rich foods, such as

FINGER FOODS FOR VERY LITTLE ONES

Some children can start eating with their fingers as early as six months (my girls weren't very skilled at it until about the nine- and ten-month mark). The following foods that I'm suggesting for young eaters are both nutritious and easy to serve. With some items, such as rice or grated cheese, you may want to press the shreds or grains into tiny lumps, to make things easier for beginning eaters.

- wedges of soft, ripe, peeled banana, peach, nectarine, melon, mango, papaya
- cooked sweet potato sticks
- wedges of cucumber, without seeds or skin
- grated carrot
- crisp crackers
- toast—spread with mashed banana for a nice treat
- bagel—served whole this makes a good teething ring
- dry cereal, unsweetened —including the ever-popular Cheerios—but avoid any cereal with nuts
- cottage cheese—in small lumps
- grated cheese
- small slices of tofu
- chopped cooked egg
- cooked rice

lean meat and cooked egg yolk. By age ten months, most children can eat adult foods, if served in a consistency they can swallow. Remember: Baby won't have all his teeth until his third birthday. Even if he does have a few teeth now, he still can't handle hard-to-chew items such as chunks of meat or wads of peanut butter and bread. Hard, raw foods such as carrots, apples and pears can be softened by partially cooking them in the microwave oven. Baby should not be eating fried foods or high-sodium items, either. Stick to plain fruits, vegetables and meats, and avoid hard, round foods such as raw carrot slices, nuts and grapes. When potentially dangerous foods such as raw carrots, whole grapes and hot dogs do become part of your child's menu, always slice them lengthwise to reduce the risk of choking. Any child under two should be supervised by an adult when eating these foods.

HEALTHY CONCERNS

HOW MUCH IS ENOUGH?

Determining how much milk or formula to feed is easy—what baby says, goes. But many parents need to know exactly how much real food to feed baby. Well, as silly as this sounds, the only one who knows the answer to that question is—once again—your child. Just as adults have times when they're hungry and times when they're not, so does your baby.

Once when my daughter Emily was about six months old, I baby-sat for my good friend Susan's daughter Candace for the first time. Emily was one month older than Candace and weighed about seven pounds more. When Susan dropped Candace off at my house, her parting words were, "Eileen, don't be surprised at Candace's lunch—she eats fast and plenty." When lunch time came, I filled each of their bowls with about a half cup of puréed fruit and started with Emily, who was bigger and therefore, I thought, hungrier. Emily ate almost all her fruit and quickly became more interested in the spoon than the food. Meanwhile, Candace was so hungry that she started shoveling the food into her mouth with both hands. She quickly emptied the first bowl. I refilled it, and *that* bowl was gone in a flash. I refilled again and again until finally, four bowls later, "little Candace," who had also eaten a full breakfast, was through with lunch.

The point is, all babies differ. Let your baby decide how much he or she needs to eat. Your job is simple: Just provide good, wholesome food in a pleasant environment. Your baby will eat if he's hungry and won't if he's not. Keep in mind, too, that it is the unusual child who is always consistent in his likes and dislikes and in the amounts he eats.

BALANCING DIET—
FROM ONE YEAR TO AGE THREE

After your baby's first birthday, you should try for a regular three-meal-a-day eating routine (plus snacks), and of course you'll want to be serving a "balanced diet." The following are daily serving suggestions that can guide you to serving healthy, well-rounded meals.

The same number of servings applies to the one-year-old as to the three-year-old—only the size of the portions will vary—depending on your child's appetite. Offer a small serving at each meal from each of the following food groups:

Milk Group—3 to 4 servings every day
Milk provides calcium, protein and riboflavin. Foods containing whole milk include formula, whole-milk yogurt, whole-milk cottage cheese, pudding made with milk and cheese. Remember, don't start cow's milk products before baby is six months of age. And don't serve low-fat dairy products before age two. Babies need fat for proper growth and development.

CALCIUM IN FOODS

The following foods contain calcium in amounts equal to 1 cup of milk:

1½ ounces Cheddar cheese	6 ounces tofu
2 cups broccoli	1¼ cups cottage cheese
1 cup yogurt	5 ounces canned salmon
1 cup custard	1½ cups ice cream

Fruits and Vegetables—4 servings every day

Fruits and vegetables provide vitamins A and C as well as fiber. You can serve baby apples, oranges, strawberries, bananas, pears, peaches, peas, green beans, potatoes, sweet potatoes and carrots, to name a few. Offer an orange or other citrus fruit every day for vitamin C and a dark-green or dark-orange vegetable every other day for vitamin A. A serving size is roughly estimated to be one to two tablespoons for each year of life. Thus, a serving of carrots for a two-year-old would be two to four tablespoons.

Meat Group—2 servings every day

Meat provides protein, iron, riboflavin, zinc and vitamin B_{12}. Sources are beef, lamb, pork, chicken, turkey, fish, beans, nut butters, tofu and eggs. A rough serving-size guide is to feed one to two tablespoons for each year of life. So when serving something like ground beef, a twelve-month-old baby needs approximately one to two tablespoons, a twenty-four-month-old needs two to four tablespoons and your three-year-old needs three to six tablespoons of cooked meat.

Grain Group—2 to 4 servings every day

Grains provide niacin, iron and thiamine. Serve baby a slice of enriched bread, preferably whole grain, half a cup of hot or cold cereal, half a cup of rice, a small bowl of enriched noodles, half a bagel, a muffin, three to six unsalted crackers or half a cup of pasta.

SNACKS

In the second year of life, the average toddler eats about five times a day: three meals and two snacks. Ideally each meal should feature all the food groups listed above, but don't drive yourself crazy trying to balance every meal perfectly. Just keep trying to serve the best meals you can. No matter how well your child eats at mealtimes, though, she may ask for snacks, too. There's nothing wrong with snacks; in fact, they help children bridge the gap between meals. Don't use them to alleviate boredom, though, or your baby will fill up and lose her appetite. Snacks should be small, nutritious, and never too sweet or salty. And when choosing a snack, keep in mind that your child doesn't share your preconceived notion about what a snack should be. For example, a cold cooked potato might not appeal to you, but to a toddler it is bite-sized, feels good in the mouth, and has a subtle, pleasant taste. Remember, too, that you're laying the groundwork for a lifetime of eating habits, so make thoughtful decisions here. Dry cereal, slices of bread, even crackers or cooked potatoes are all good choices. All too soon your child will learn about chips, soda and candy.

SALT

Added table salt has *no place* in your baby's diet for three reasons: (1) Sodium is present *naturally* in vegetables, grains and even water; (2) too much sodium at an early age can predispose your baby to high blood pressure in adulthood; and (3) the taste for salt is acquired. If baby develops a taste for salt as an infant, he probably won't be able to break it. The last thing you want to do is raise a child who can't eat anything without smothering it with salt first.

Keeping sodium intake low is easy if baby's menu consists of fresh, unprocessed foods. Plain fruit, meats and vegetables contain very little sodium. Eggs, fruit juices, unsalted crackers, rice, noodles, pasta and cereals are also low. On the other hand, convenience foods such as canned vegetables, soups, frozen dinners and commercial rice and noodle mixes are all loaded with added salt.

Studies show that as baby starts to eat foods from the table, his sodium intake can easily skyrocket. Adult foods such as luncheon meats and canned combination dishes like beef stew or spaghetti sauce can contribute significantly. So serve your baby fresh or frozen meats without salt, such as chicken, beef or lamb, and plain fresh or frozen vegetables instead of those with salty sauces. Fresh fruits or those canned in their own juices are also fine. Cheese, however, is high in sodium, so use it sparingly.

ON TOP OF SPAGHETTI

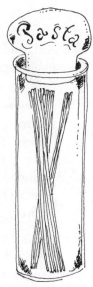

As every mother knows, kids love tomato sauces and canned spaghetti dishes. A good tomato sauce, poured over spaghetti and served with a piece of cheese or some cottage cheese, is a great one-dish meal. But canned spaghetti and tomato sauces can be loaded with sodium, and I think children should learn at the beginning that food tastes best *without* a lot of salt. So read labels carefully, and find a tomato purée or tomato sauce that's made with just tomatoes and water—and no added salt. The no-added-salt tomato purée that I've found comes in a thirty-two-ounce can. I open the can, use what I need, then freeze the rest in half-cup portions in plastic containers and thaw them in a microwave-safe dish as needed. Don't refrigerate sauce in the can. Recently I discovered an eight-ounce can of no-added-salt tomato sauce that not only tastes good but also eliminates the need for the thirty-two-ounce can of plain purée. Make the effort to hunt out these products in your supermarket —it's definitely worth your time.

A COMPARISON OF SODIUM IN TOMATO PRODUCTS

The sodium level rises as the tomato becomes more processed, and the same holds true for most vegetables and convenience foods.

Tomato	Sodium in Milligrams
1 raw	4
purée, no salt added (1 cup)	105 *
catsup (1 tablespoon)	156
canned whole (1 cup)	313
juice (1 cup)	486
purée, canned with salt (1 cup)	905

Source: USDA Handbook 456
* product label

IRON

Iron-deficiency anemia is the most common nutrition problem in young children. In fact, 10 percent of American toddlers have it. If your pregnancy was healthy and you ate well, then your baby was probably born with an adequate supply of iron—enough to last for the first six months of life. After six months, though, these iron stores are insufficient for further growth and baby must get iron from food.

Just one serving of iron-fortified infant cereal provides half the iron your baby needs for the day. Meat, poultry, liver and egg yolks are also good sources. To minimize the chances of iron deficiency, vary your baby's diet and carefully monitor his intake of iron (see chart). Don't serve more than one quart of milk a day, because too much milk (which is iron-poor) can diminish appetite and prevent baby from eating other, iron-rich foods.

Serving vitamin C–rich foods with each meal will also enhance your baby's iron absorption. Sources include oranges, berries and even tomatoes. And when baby graduates from infant cereals, there are plenty of adult cereals that contain iron. Read the labels and look for one that provides at least 45 percent of the RDA.

IRON CONTENT OF SELECTED FOODS

The Recommended Dietary Allowance (RDA) for babies six months to age three is 10 milligrams per day.

	Iron in Milligrams	Percentage of USRDA		Iron in Milligrams	Percentage of USRDA
beef liver (8 ounces)	20	200	potato (1)	1.1	11
chicken liver (8 ounces)	19	190	peach (1, no skin)	.7	7
iron-fortified infant cereal (3 tablespoons)	6.6	66	peanut butter (1 tablespoon)	.3	3
pork (1 cup)	4.5	45	milk (1 cup, whole)	.1	1
kidney beans (1 cup)	4.6	46	Cheddar cheese (1 ounce)	.3	3
lentils (1 cup)	4.2	42			
spinach (1 cup)	4.0	40			
beef (1 cup)	3.7	37	*Baby Foods*		
prune juice (⅓ cup)	3.5	35	beef (3.5 ounces)	2.0	20
lamb (1 cup)	2.4	24	chicken (3.5 ounces)	1.9	19
turkey (1 cup)	2.5	25	egg yolk (3.5 ounces)	2.8	28
chicken (1 cup)	1.8	18	beef noodle dinner (3.5 ounces)	.35	4
halibut (8 ounces)	1.6	16	chicken noodle dinner (3.5 ounces)	.35	4
applesauce (1 cup)	1.5	15			

Source: USDA Handbook 456

SUPERMARKET SAVVY

Despite its attractions, you won't be cooking everything your baby eats in the microwave. You'll still be buying bread, crackers and the like, and you can turn your supermarket into a health-food store by being a smart shopper. Feeding a baby can be a great opportunity for your whole family to look at how and what they eat. Many new parents find that *they* start eating better because they buy healthy foods for baby and eat more regular meals. The best foods to buy for baby—and in general—are those that food companies have tampered with the least. Choose plain meat, vegetables, eggs, 100 percent fruit juice, unsalted crackers, plain rice, noodles or pasta, cereal without added sugar, whole wheat bread, plain yogurt, fresh meat and poultry. Frozen dinners and canned vegetables contain too much salt—even for toddlers.

As a rule, convenience foods are frequently loaded with fat and salt, but there are a few exceptions, such as plain frozen vegetables and frozen plain cheese ravioli. Frozen vegetables are "flash" frozen after harvest and can actually contain more nutrition than fresh vegetables that are old and wilted. When deciding if a food belongs on your baby's menu, ask yourself if it has added salt, sugar or preservatives. If the answer is yes, *don't* buy it for baby.

THE WELL-STOCKED PANTRY

What follows are ideas that will keep you from ever uttering those dreadful words: "There's nothing to feed the baby!" Many of these foods can be put on the table in minutes—no chopping, no fussing, no panic and no tears. So when you lose track of time and lunch is an hour overdue, it's very nice to walk into the kitchen, pull something out of the freezer or cupboard, put it in the microwave and cook it while you wash little hands and put a bib on baby. The idea here is that you can always have at least a one-day emergency supply of appropriate, simple foods on hand, and once you use them, you restock quickly. Try my suggestions, and I'm sure you will come up with good ideas of your own. If you see foods you don't usually cook, then you and your baby will have some pleasant surprises in store. Recipes for foods like rice and vegetables are all in My Top One Hundred (see page 65). I have not included commercial jars of baby food, but you certainly can. The important thing is always to have something on hand. There is nothing wrong with grabbing a jar of ready-to-eat baby food, particularly when you are really rushed.

IN THE BEGINNING (0 TO 4 MONTHS)

Formula
The breast-fed baby needs only ready access to Mom, and for formula-fed babies, just keep a ready supply of formula on hand. The equivalent of 30 to 40 ounces of formula, starting from either liquid or powder, is about the right-size "emergency supply."

This is roughly how much a baby can drink in a day.

ONCE SOLIDS START (4 TO 6 MONTHS)

Formula

Keep large quantities on hand, either dry or liquid, enough to feed baby up to 40 ounces a day, if this is what baby is drinking. Even for breast-fed babies, a can of formula powder is handy to have around, particularly for mixing with cereal.

Infant Cereal

Keep a box each of iron-fortified rice, oatmeal and barley cereal.

Fruit

Keep infant juice and a few jars of infant fruit on hand.

A LITTLE MORE INTERESTING (6 TO 10 MONTHS)

Formula

Powder or ready-made.

Milk

Babies can start on cow's milk as early as six months if they are eating other solid foods, too. But until baby makes the switch, always keep plenty of formula on hand. Canned evaporated milk can be especially helpful on those mornings when you completely run out of fresh whole milk. Mix canned milk with equal portions of water before serving, and of course serve only after baby has tried cow's milk and had no allergic reaction.

Infant Cereal

Cream of wheat and oatmeal are both appealing at this age. These two are usually not iron fortified, so don't make them baby's regular cereal.

Juice

Bottles of infant juice or frozen apple (Alar-free), white grape and orange juice (after eight months). I serve only the clear juices to cut down on staining. Babies love vitamin C–fortified grape juice and cranberry juice, but what a mess they can make!

Frozen Vegetables

Buy the big plastic bags, which are easiest to take small portions from and are often less expensive. Most babies like carrots, green beans, peas and spinach.

Canned Fruits

Buy the kind without sugar added. Try peaches, pears, mandarin oranges and applesauce.

Grains

Keep barley, rice (brown and white), dry noodles and pasta.

BABY MOVES TO ADULT FOODS (10 TO 36 MONTHS)

Milk
Canned evaporated milk and formula (if you're still using it).

Cereal
Keep two varieties on hand—infant type and any dry cereal without nuts or added sugar, preferably iron fortified.

Crackers
Keep at least one of the following kinds of crackers in the cupboard to quell active appetites: grahams, unsalted saltines, rice cakes, bread sticks.

Juice
Always have at least one day's juice supply in reserve. It could be a frozen juice concentrate, an unopened bottled juice or boxes of juice concentrate that just need water. Try to serve only 100 percent fruit juice.

Fruit
Keep one or two cans of fruit (no sugar added), a jar of applesauce and dried fruit (raisins, apricots and dates).

Vegetables
Keep at least two frozen vegetables on hand at all times, one dark green (maybe peas, which almost all babies eat with gusto) and one deep orange (squash is our household favorite), as well as potatoes and onions. Also have canned tomato purée or whole tomatoes, preferably the no-added-salt variety.

Protein Foods
Keep one can of kidney beans (which need no additional cooking, but need rinsing before serving to get rid of salt). In the freezer keep uncooked small portions of ground beef, turkey, lamb and pork. Cheese, eggs, peanut butter and dried beans such as lentils can all be quick, healthy protein foods.

Grains
Barley, rice, kasha, millet, couscous.

Macaroni
Orzo, egg noodles, spaghetti, lasagna noodles.

Jell-O
For sick days.

Extras from the Frozen-Food Case
There are a few foods I buy regularly that are good for you, and convenient, too. These include:
frozen cheese raviolis
bean burritos (no preservatives or additives)
waffles
plain pizza crusts (Topped with cheese, vegetables and tomatoes, these make nutritious pizzas in ten minutes.)

Tofu Pups. These are hot dogs made with tofu. They are much lower in fat and sodium than the usual version, and they taste good, too, though not exactly like a hot dog. Just prick the skin and heat for 45 seconds in the microwave oven at 100 percent power.

AT A GLANCE: AN INFANT AND TODDLER FEEDING GUIDE

I developed this chart to be used as a quick meal planner. Don't be a slave to it. Use it as a general guide. Month by month I've listed which foods to introduce, and suggested amounts and what consistency to serve them in. From birth to four months, nothing but breast milk or formula needs to be on the menu. At four to six months, try cereal mixed with formula, expressed milk or infant apple juice. In the six- to eight-month period, offer small amounts of any of the foods listed. You'll notice that I haven't given specific portion sizes because at this age baby is just learning to eat and still getting most of his nutrition from milk.

Your baby's need for food will increase after the eighth month, and now you will want to work your way toward a more complete menu. When baby reaches the ten- to twelve-month range, he will be able to eat small portions of almost any food, provided you mince or chop it. His consumption of milk will drop off now, making room for the introduction of many new foods. By his first birthday he'll be eating most of the foods you enjoy. From twelve to thirty-six months his food needs will be similar to yours: three meals a day plus nutritious snacks. Your baby should eat all food groups daily, the only difference from your diet being the amounts.

EVEN THE BEST-LAID PLANS...

The toast is burned. The baby spills breakfast all over the rug. The coffeemaker's on the fritz. You have a fight with your husband. You leave the baby screaming in your sitter's arms as you walk out the door. Why me, you ask? Well, parents, you're not alone. We don't all start our days with a leisurely breakfast, thirty minutes of friendly chitchat and a passionate kiss good-bye. So don't be discouraged if your ideal vision of parenthood, formed while pregnant, has turned out—in reality—quite differently.

Having children challenges your patience, organization, understanding, even old family traditions. And mealtime challenges start the day you bring baby home.

Even *before* your baby is eating she will probably be able to disrupt your suppers. For a while David and I called our daughter "Emily the food detector," because she'd always cry and fuss when we sat down to eat.

You're not dealing with adults here, so don't expect things to be predictable. Most adults have a common mealtime goal: eating good food in a pleasant family environment. Unfortunately, children don't always share these goals. They want good food, but *good* can mean mushed and squished and spread around before eaten. To you a pleasant environment might mean a clean table and clean hands. To your toddler it might mean standing in the high chair and making a waterfall with his milk or spitting food at an older sibling.

CREATING A PLEASANT MEALTIME

If you create a happy mealtime from the start, your baby will eat better and develop good eating habits. And this will make your life a lot easier. Here are some dos and don'ts for making mealtimes pleasant, based on my own experience as well as on advice culled from seasoned parents.

Mealtimes are messy, so be prepared. Always plan ahead. Try to have everything you'll need ready on the table—napkins, cups, bowls, spoons, seconds on juice and bread and, of course, the main meal—so that you won't have to leave baby. *Don't* put Johnny in a nice clean outfit before mealtime; instead, wait until after he's eaten. *Don't* put on *your* nice new silk blouse for work and then sit down to feed little Jenny. *Don't* leave your brand-new, or even old, wall-to-wall carpeting in the dining room— or eating area—unprotected. Cover rugs or flooring with newspaper or plastic for easy cleanup. *Do* give baby enough space at the table so that he can't reach your food. *Do* make rules and stick to them. In our house, for example, toys cannot be played with until after meals are finished.

The thing that's saved me the most time is always having food ready. When kids are hungry, you can't expect them to wait thirty minutes, or at least not to wait quietly. Waiting when hungry means crying—and driving you crazy. With this in mind, I designed most of the recipes to be made and on the table within fifteen minutes. But for a hungry child, even *that* may be too long. Try serving a small snack to stop the crying. I usually serve something that might go with supper anyway, such as a slice of bread or a piece of fruit. Keep these small, though, or the main meal won't be eaten.

Everyone wonders about table manners. My advice is pick your battles and be realistic. It's surprising how early children learn to develop good or bad habits. First, remember that the apple never falls far from the tree. If you sit at the table, use a napkin and ask for food politely. Eventually this will rub off on your child. My rule for table behavior is simple but practical. Whenever Sarah or Emily does something I have a problem with, I ask myself if I can live with it. For example: Sarah eats faster than David or

INFANT FEEDING GUIDE*

Food Form	0–4 Months Liquid	4–6 Months Strained	6–8 Months Strained, Mashed
Breast milk Formula Cow's milk	5–10 feedings 16–32 ounces none	4–7 feedings 24–40 ounces none	3–4 feedings 24–32 ounces can be introduced
Cereals and bread	none	infant cereal: rice, oatmeal, barley. Mix with water, juice, formula or breast milk.	all varieties of infant cereal (none with honey, nuts or dried fruit), teething biscuit
Fruit juice	none	infant juice with added vitamin C	infant juice with vitamin C (try a cup)
Vegetables	none	none	strained or mashed cooked vegetables (not corn; offer dark green or dark orange every other day)
Fruit	none	none	fresh or cooked fruit—mash or purée (no skins, peels or seeds)
Protein	none	none	try plain yogurt

*Consult your pediatrician or registered dietitian for specific amounts.

TODDLER FEEDING GUIDE*

Food Form	8–10 Months Mashed, Minced Fine	10–12 Months Minced, Chopped	12–36 Months Chopped, Table Food
Breast milk Formula Cow's milk	3–4 feedings *or* 16–24 ounces *or* 16–24 ounces	3–4 feedings *or* 16–24 ounces *or* 16–24 ounces	2–3 feedings *or* 2–4 servings of milk or other calcium-rich foods: yogurt, cottage cheese, tofu, green leafy vegetables
Cereals and breads	infant cereal, cream of wheat, oatmeal, toast, bagel, plain crackers 2–3 servings daily	infant cereal and all varieties of unsweetened cereal, bread, rice, noodles, crackers, spaghetti 2–4 servings daily	infant cereal or other unsweetened cereal, all whole-grain or enriched pasta, rice, bread 4 servings daily (about ⅓ of adult portion)
Fruit juice	all 100 percent juice—try orange or tomato 4 ounces vitamin C–rich juice daily	all 100 percent juice—orange, grapefruit and pineapple are good choices 4 ounces vitamin C–rich daily	all 100 percent juice—avoid those with sugar 4 ounces vitamin C–rich juice daily
Vegetables	most cooked or mashed 1–2 servings daily	cooked, some raw: tomatoes, seeded cucumber slices 1–2 servings daily	all varieties, cooked or raw (if sliced or prepared, to match chewing ability) 2 servings daily

*Consult your pediatrician or registered dietitian for specific amounts.

TODDLER FEEDING GUIDE*

Food Form	8–10 Months Mashed, Minced Fine	10–12 Months Minced, Chopped	12–36 Months Chopped, Table Food
Fruit	fresh or cooked—try soft, ripe banana, peaches, pears, oranges 1–2 servings daily	all fruits, peeled and seeded, canned—no sugar added 1–2 servings daily	all fruits—offer a citrus fruit daily 2 servings daily
Protein	lean meat, chicken or fish; egg yolks; plain yogurt; dried beans; peanut butter; cottage cheese 1–2 tablespoons daily	lamb, beef, pork, fish or poultry; eggs; cheese; yogurt; beans; tofu; peanut butter 1–2 tablespoons twice a day	all meat, fish or poultry; eggs, nut butters; beans; tofu 2 servings daily (at least ½-ounce portion)

*Consult your pediatrician or registered dietitian for specific amounts.

me. Sure, I'd like her to stay seated with us, but once she's finished, she can't sit still and wants to get down. That's fine with me, until she gets in my lap while I'm still eating. That's when I say *no*.

Setting limits is tough the first time, but it makes life run more smoothly and living with a child *much* more pleasant. Taking action early will pay dividends in the future. It is also important to have other adults or older children back you up on rules. In my experience, setting rules is most important between fifteen and twenty-four months of age.

Remember, too, that the behavior you allow at home must also be acceptable in restaurants or at Grandma's house. It's not fair to let your child dance on the table at home, then yell at her for doing the same thing when you go to your in-laws.

MAKING MANNERS STICK

To enforce rules, attach consequences to breaking them. If Sarah is using her spoon to play with food, I might say, "Stop playing with your spoon or I'll take it away." And if she keeps playing with it, I *do* take it away. Idle threats will get you nowhere. Your baby might cry, but she will also know that you mean business, and this strategy will reward you in the long run. The trick to success is making the consequences reasonable. Threatening your child with an hour in the playpen for playing with her spoon is clearly not reasonable, and you wouldn't be able to make it stick.

SCHEDULES

Most young children actually like schedules. So keep a schedule, but be flexible, too. Breakfast time in our house varies widely, depending on if it's a weekend or a workday. But lunch is almost always at noon and supper around five o'clock. Our children seem to thrive on the predictability of a schedule and are much more likely to tolerate exceptions if meals usually come at the same time. Having a schedule lets you have fun with snacks, too. Of course snacks should be nutritious, but think of the fun and pure pleasure an unexpected ice cream can bring at two in the afternoon. Sure, a toddler full of ice cream might not eat as much at supper, but as long as you're giving her healthy meals, don't worry. She ate a good breakfast and lunch, and tomorrow you'll give her a lighter snack. I do take nutrition seriously, but it's silly to think that just one meal or snack determines the quality of a child's diet. It's the overall picture, the combination of meals and snacks over time.

SWEETS

You may wonder why, despite all your efforts —calling candy "junk" or filling your child with healthy food—your child has a craving for sweets. Well, the taste for sweets is innate, so there really isn't much you can do. Here are some guidelines I use to keep my children's sweet teeth under control: Don't give sweets at every demand. Time them appropriately, because they do affect appetite. Also, give them for the taste pleasure they provide and not as rewards or punishments for behavior. And whenever possible, serve sweets that are also nutritious. All the desserts in the recipe section are designed with nutritional value in mind. Hint: Cooking intensifies the sweetness in fresh fruit, so try serving cooked apples, pears, peaches or bananas for a healthy, satisfying treat.

THE CLEAN PLATE CLUB

Please don't force children to finish everything you serve them. The truth is, *You don't know how much they need.* I once had a baby-sitter who proudly told me she didn't give Emily her peaches because she didn't drink all her milk. To her surprise, I asked her not to do that again, because I felt that only Emily knew if Emily was thirsty.

WHAT TO DO WHEN BABY "JUST SAYS NO"

Sometimes it's hard to keep toddlers from too much snacking, but what do you do when your child won't eat? Here are the top ten reasons my kids won't eat. Maybe they'll apply to your children, too.

1. They're not hungry.
2. They're sick.
3. They're upset about something.
4. They ate a snack or had a drink too close to supper.
5. The food is too hot, or they think it is too hot.
6. They want attention.
7. They are suspicious of the food—it looks funny.
8. The food is "out of order"; perhaps a pea has strayed into the potatoes.
9. The food feels funny in the mouth.
10. The food doesn't taste good.

You can easily rule out sickness by checking your child's temperature and trying to find out if his tummy or any other area hurts. Think back. Is he constipated or is diarrhea a problem? If your child continues to have no appetite, don't hesitate to check with your doctor. Illness can cause your child to lose interest in food. If your child is in good health and still won't eat, consider the following tactics:

1. Give your child the benefit of the doubt and assume he has a reason and try to figure it out.
2. If your child can talk, let him tell you why he won't eat.
3. Look at yourself. If refusing foods gets a specific response from you, baby may be doing it to get you to respond in that manner.
4. Trust yourself and your child. A healthy child will eat when hungry, and one meal refused won't do any damage.

FOOD FOR THOUGHT

If you feel a growing stressful relationship with your child around food, do something about it. Seek out a dietitian or even a family therapist for feeding advice. Or head for the library. In an excellent book called *Child of Mine: Feeding with Love & Good Sense* by Ellyn Satter, R.D., the author talks in detail about coping with eating problems and disorders. And here's one last observation from a mother on the front line: Children are stress meters. When there's a disruption in the house, expect disruptive behavior. I've learned that my children cause me the least stress and are most pleasant when I'm giving them all my attention. As soon as I try to make some phone calls, clean the house or even just do my nails, that's when my kids —and I—get frustrated.

Does this mean you can't live *your* life? Of course not. But it does mean that there will often be stress in your family. So learn to accept the change your children have brought. It's all part of being a family.

Keep in mind, too, that the intense attention required by young children is temporary. Within ten years they're in junior high and have a life of their own. Time goes by all too quickly. So, despite the stresses, annoyances and general turmoil you're going through, try to enjoy having a little one who depends on you and looks to you for love and comfort.

4

INTO THE MOUTHS OF BABES

 Once you get over the initial hurdle of introducing solid foods to your children, you run up against the more sophisticated health issues. Cholesterol, obesity, allergies, sodium, vegetarianism and pesticides are just a few of the concerns that plague new parents. What you feed your baby is essential to his health, but it's important to remember that a diet designed for a healthy adult does not necessarily apply to your baby. A case in point: Skim milk may be good for you, but baby needs whole milk for proper brain development.

DON'T GO OVERBOARD

In 1987 a New York doctor, Michael T. Pugliese, discovered seven cases of malnutrition caused by well-meaning parents. These parents had feared that their children, ranging from seven to twenty-two months, might develop health problems on a conventional diet. So, in an effort to prevent obesity and heart disease, they cut back on calories and fat by diluting formula, restricting foods and snacks and serving low-fat milk. These parents did *not* cause malnutrition out of neglect. They loved their children and thought they were doing the right thing. But instead of improving their babies' health, the diet caused poor growth and inadequate weight gain. Happily, once the children returned to a conventional diet, they all regained their health.

The point is that while what a child eats in infancy and toddlerhood is extremely important, the principles of good nutrition that apply to adults may not apply to babies and young children. Babies and children are constantly growing, and their needs for nutrients are different from those of adults who are fully grown.

A good rule of thumb when evaluating any dietary practice is to ask yourself, does this diet go to extremes? If you're eliminating whole food groups from your baby's menu or serving large quantities of just one food daily, please reevaluate the diet, because you may be hurting your growing child.

On the pages that follow you'll read about all sorts of health problems, many of them preventable. This chapter is intended to give you some reassurance and to provide you with information to set your child off on the right foot.

OBESITY

The health issue that concerned me most when I started feeding Sarah was obesity. At every new meeting with friends or relatives, especially when they hadn't seen her for a while, their comments were always the same: "Boy, she's a *big* baby." It was true. Sarah had cuffs of soft chubby fat around her wrists and thighs and so many rolls of fat around her tummy that my husband affectionately dubbed her "the Michelin tire baby."

At six months she was still nursing four to five times a day but eating only a few spoonfuls of food at any given meal, and she was very chubby. Even though she was thriving on Mother Nature's recipe, I was still worried about her "fatness." But at her six-month checkup, both her height and weight were in the ninety-fifth percentile. She was a big baby, but her weight wasn't out of proportion to her height. Today, at two and a half, her baby fat has diminished, and she's a lean, busy toddler.

The good news for chubby infants like Sarah is that there's little correlation between the weight of infants in the first six months and what they'll weigh after two years. In the first six months of a baby's life, weight is more a reflection of how the mother ate while pregnant and not of what baby is eating now. Trying to fight or prevent obesity by restricting food at too early an age is likely to cause more trouble than happiness. Even if your baby appears chubby, *do not* restrict his food intake. Lay down guidelines for snacks and meals, and allow him to satisfy his appetite with nutritious foods.

If you're still concerned after baby turns two, consult your doctor, who may refer you to a nutritionist. But don't put your young child on a diet without proper supervision and sound advice.

Delaying solid foods until four to six months is often credited with preventing obesity, but more and more the experts are disagreeing. One theory says that if you introduce solid food too soon, your baby's caloric consumption will increase significantly because he will be consuming both the milk feeding and solid food, too. Other scientists now say that the introduction of solids will automatically cut back on the amount of milk consumed, thus keeping calories at the level baby needs. Of course, you should delay solids until at least four months anyway, when baby will be developmentally ready for them.

A NOTE ABOUT TV AND OBESITY

Dr. William Dietz of the New England Medical Center in Boston has discovered a correlation between the amount of television children watch and obesity. So whenever possible, steer your child toward active play instead of television. Dr. Dietz prefers increased activity over dietary deprivation for controlling and preventing weight problems.

ALLERGIES

If you or your spouse has food allergies, your child is likely to have them, too. But there is something you can do. Try to breast-feed your baby as long as possible, and don't introduce cow's milk until at least six months. Stay on formula instead. Hold off on solids until at least four months, and then make sure you try each new food individually,

ALLERGY VERSUS REACTION

All too frequently we label a food reaction as an allergy. Food reactions are less serious than allergies and are usually accompanied by short-lived symptoms. A true food allergy involves the immune system and, if present, can be serious and require special medical tests and treatment. When Dr. S. Allen Bock of Denver, Colorado, looked for food intolerances in a study of 480 children, he found that the majority of food reactions were likely to occur in the first year of life but would be gone by baby's third birthday. Diarrhea, vomiting, skin rashes, colic and nasal congestion were the most common confirmed symptoms in this young group of children. What is important here is that this study found that few if any of the adverse reactions reported by the children and parents were true food allergies.

❋   ❋   ❋

waiting five days before adding a new one. Avoid the typical problem foods, listed below, until at least nine months.

In the first year of life, particularly between the fourth and ninth months, your child is at a greater risk for allergies because his digestive system is not fully developed. Add a new cereal, fruit or vegetable to your baby's diet and you suddenly find a skin rash or unexplained diarrhea. The new food may be the culprit, and if so, you should temporarily avoid it. Egg white, cow's milk, fish, peanuts, wheat, chicken, soybeans and citrus fruits are all likely troublemakers. But if these foods cause problems, that doesn't mean you'll have to skip them forever. Try a small amount in about a month and take heart in knowing that most children outgrow early allergies to most foods, except nut and fish allergies (which tend to be permanent), by their third birthday.

FOODS MOST LIKELY TO CAUSE ALLERGIES

cow's milk	fish
eggs	shellfish
nuts	

Other Possible Problem Foods

wheat	citrus fruits
corn	peas
berries	beans
certain spices	

MILK ALLERGY

The good news is that fewer than eight out of one hundred infants are allergic to cow's milk. That statistic is of little comfort, however, if your baby happens to be one of the eight. An allergy to milk occurs when an infant's immune system produces antibodies that attack the cow's milk protein. Symptoms can include chronic diarrhea, abdominal cramps, vomiting, even wheezing and eczema.

On the recommendation of a doctor, formula-fed babies with milk allergy can switch to formulas that use soybeans as a protein source (Nursoy, ProSobee, Mull-Soyfor and Isomil are examples). If your baby is allergic to soy protein too, then formulas such as Nutramigen, Pregestimil and Alimentum are products that have "predigested" protein, which are tolerated better by children who have a milk allergy.

Breast-feeding mothers usually don't have to worry about milk allergy, but studies have found that some mothers who drink large quantities of milk can pass cow's milk protein into breast milk. If your breast-fed baby is allergic to cow's milk protein and *you* are drinking a lot of milk, *he* might exhibit allergic symptoms. The solution is not to stop breast-feeding. Instead, limit milk to the recommended four servings per day and consider drinking it in several small servings. And be sure to try to get enough calcium from nonmilk sources.

Don't decide your baby has milk allergy without talking to your health-care provider. If milk allergy is not the cause of your

WHICH IS IT?

One other note: Lactose intolerance (also known as milk sugar intolerance) is often confused with milk allergy. Milk intolerance is the body's inability to digest the carbohydrate in milk called lactose. Symptoms can include diarrhea, cramping and gas. Milk allergy results in an allergic reaction that involves the immune system. It's important to distinguish between the two so you can start the right remedy. Once again, the good news is that infants very rarely suffer from lactose intolerance. If lactose is a problem, it can be avoided by drinking Lactaid milk and lactose-free formulas and eating Lactaid cheese products. For more information, contact: Lactaid, Sugarlo Company, Atlantic City, NJ 08404.

baby's symptoms, you need to find out what is. If it is the cause, symptoms should stop within forty-eight hours of stopping milk and reappear when milk is reintroduced.

Contrary to popular belief, a child who is allergic to cow's milk may also be allergic to goat's milk. Also, boiling milk will not make it safe for the allergic child to drink.

The good news is that most children outgrow milk allergies by two or three years of age. For information on cooking without milk, see the appendix.

BITING OFF MORE THAN BABY CAN CHEW

What do hot dogs, candy and grapes have in common? They all can cause your child to choke. A 1984 report in *The Journal of the American Medical Association* found that these three foods alone were responsible for *40 percent* of all the food-related choking deaths in young children. Most of us don't realize how serious and common a problem choking on food is. We've all heard plenty of warnings about protecting our children from accidental poisonings, but for every child who dies each year in the United States from accidental poisoning (seventy-five), another dies from choking on food.

FOODS THAT MIGHT CAUSE CHOKING (SERVE WITH CARE)

hot dogs	meat, poultry or fish	carrots
nuts	with bones	peanut butter
cookies	seeds	bread
apples	shrimp	gum
popcorn	hard, round candy	cheese
beans	grapes	peas
noodles	meat	cherries with pits

Your child is much more likely to choke than you are for several reasons. First, his airway is smaller and his gag reflex, which might dislodge food, is weaker. Second, children aren't careful eaters. They may talk, laugh, even run while eating, and are often more distracted at mealtime than other, older members of the family.

To prevent choking, *always* supervise mealtimes carefully and *never* allow a young child to eat alone. Foods that are small, thin, smooth or slick when wet, or hard and tough are all potential troublemakers. When serving such foods, always cut, chop or break them up into manageable pieces. For example, always slice hot dogs and grapes lengthwise, and don't let your toddlers eat hard, round candies such as sourballs. LifeSavers, because they're thin and smaller, are a better bet.

Any parent who has had to save a choking child knows the meaning of the word *terror*. It's most important to act quickly, and it will help if you know exactly what to do. Read and practice the guidelines opposite, post a copy in a readily accessible spot, and teach the procedure to your baby-sitter. Ask your day-care center if all the workers know how to treat a choking child, and if they don't, offer to teach them or ask the local hospital, Red Cross or fire department to give a class.

Choking

Begin the following if the child is choking and is unable to breathe. If the child is coughing, crying, or speaking, **DO NOT** do any of the following, but call your doctor for further advice.

FOR INFANTS UNDER ONE YEAR OLD (A)

- Call for emergency services or 911.
- Place infant face down over your arm with head lower than the trunk. Rest your forearm on your thigh.
- Deliver four blows with the heel of the hand, striking high between the infant's shoulder blades.
- If blockage is not relieved, roll the infant over. Lay the child down, face up, on a firm surface. Give four rapid chest compressions over the breastbone using two fingers.
- If the above measures have not removed the blockage, open mouth with thumb over tongue and fingers wrapped around lower jaw.
- If you can see the foreign body, remove it with a sideways sweep of a finger. (Never poke your finger straight into the throat.)

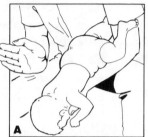

Be careful, though, because finger sweeps may push the object further down the airway.

- If blockage is not relieved and the child cannot breathe, begin the technique of pulmonary support **(D)**, outlined in the opposite column.
- Rapid transport to a medical facility is urgent if these emergency first aid measures fail.

FOR CHILDREN OVER ONE YEAR OLD

- Call for emergency services or 911.
- Place child on his back. Kneel at the child's feet. Put the heel of one hand on the child's abdomen in the midline between the navel and rib cage. Place the second hand on top of the first. **(B)**
- The older, larger child can be treated in a sitting, standing, or recumbent position. **(C)**
- Press firmly, but gently, into the abdomen with a rapid inward and upward thrust. Repeat six to ten times. These abdominal thrusts – called the Heimlich maneuver – should be applied until the foreign body is expelled.
- If the above measures have not removed the blockage, open mouth with thumb over tongue and fingers wrapped around lower jaw.
- If you can see the foreign body, remove it with a sideways sweep of a finger. (Never poke your finger straight into the throat.)

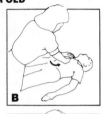

Be careful, though, because finger sweeps may push the object further down the airway.

- If blockage is not relieved and the child cannot breathe, begin the technique of pulmonary support **(D)**, outlined in the opposite column.
- Rapid transport to a medical facility is urgent if these emergency first aid measures fail.

Cardio Pulmonary Resuscitation (CPR)

To be used in situations such as drowning, electric shock and smoke inhalation or when breathing or heartbeat stops.

TECHNIQUE OF PULMONARY SUPPORT (D)

Begin the following if the child is not breathing:

- Place victim on back.
- Straighten neck (unless neck injury suspected) and lift jaw.
- Give slow steady breaths into infant's nose and mouth and into larger child's mouth with nostrils pinched closed.
- Breathe at 20 breaths per minute for infants and 15 breaths per minute for children, using only enough air to move chest up and down.

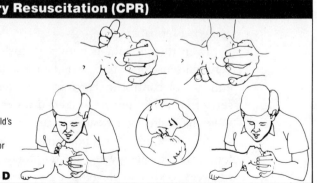

SOURCE: American Academy of Pediatrics

TASTE: THE GATEKEEPER

Wouldn't it be wonderful to understand exactly how your baby tastes the food you feed him? That way you could serve just the foods you know he'll like. Unfortunately, though, not all babies taste the same way. When two children eat the same food, their sensory experiences can be completely different. Any mother of more than one child can confirm this: Sometimes it's impossible to make a meal everybody likes.

What we do know about taste is that most babies like sweet things. To many parents this might be a source of concern, but it shouldn't be. The taste for sweets is innate. And it also may be nature's way of helping babies select substances that contain calories, and it may protect them from swallowing poisons or other harmful foods. After all, foods that naturally contain sugar, such as fruit and milk, are generally wholesome and good for baby.

Even though baby is born with his own personal sense of taste, it may be possible to enhance or control it. For instance, studies show that babies given sweetened water are more likely to prefer sugar than children given plain water. If this holds true for other foods, then babies given a greater proportion of sweet foods may develop a greater sweet tooth than children who get more calories from nonsweetened foods.

So don't automatically worry if your baby likes sweets. It's natural. What you should worry about is how you meet this taste. It's best to give your little ones *naturally* sweet foods. Apples, bananas, plums, even squash and sweet potatoes are tasty, and these foods also carry lots of nutrition. On the other hand, simple sugars such as white and brown sugar, corn syrups and honey have no place in a very young child's diet. These foods carry very few nutrients, and adding them to your baby's diet at an early age may make your baby too accustomed to having sweets as part of his regular diet. Honey poses another threat because it could carry tiny botulism spores that only affect infants. When a child is fifteen months or older and eating three meals a day plus snacks, then you can safely serve foods with added sugar, providing that baby eats nonsweetened foods, too, and that they don't interfere with meals.

Once you've acknowledged that your child will almost certainly have a sweet tooth, try to work with it. For instance, if you want your baby to eat green beans and you're serving applesauce, too, you may have better success if you give the green beans first and follow them with the sweeter fruit. I personally don't have a problem with giving young children vegetables mixed with fruit. If you mix mashed bananas with peas and it gets baby to eat them, *fine*. As baby gets older, he'll learn to eat them plain, too.

Salt is another taste that concerns parents, particularly since a diet high in salt is linked with high blood pressure. Babies are *not* born with a taste for salt. But as they grow older—even as early as four months—they may develop a preference for salty foods. Scientists are still arguing about whether the taste for salt is learned with age or develops inherently as taste matures. Adults' taste for salt can increase with heavy use, and the same may hold true for babies. So don't add salt to your cooking. By avoiding the heavy use of salt or presalted foods, you may be able to control and even prevent a strong taste for salt when your baby grows up.

VEGETARIAN NUTRITION

A vegetarian diet should not be given to a young child casually. Babies need adequate protein and calories. Without them growth and development will be stunted. Protein is easily obtained from animal foods such as eggs, milk, cheese, fish, poultry, beef and pork. So if you are a vegetarian, the degree of restriction in your diet will influence how

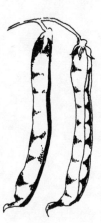

careful you must be in planning your child's diet.

If you choose to eliminate only red meats such as pork and beef but still serve fish, poultry, milk and eggs, then the protein from the red meat is easily replaced. If, however, you eliminate *all* animal foods including milk, eggs and cheese, it will be virtually impossible for your baby to get the necessary protein and vitamin B_{12} she needs. Fat and iron intake may also be too low. Babies and adults both need to take carefully planned supplements of B_{12} if all animal sources of protein are eliminated from their menus.

A vegetarian diet may be too low in calories, too, and *babies need calories*. Meat, poultry and eggs offer calories in a concentrated source. If they're eliminated, your baby will need to eat *extra* amounts of foods such as vegetables and grains, amounts that may be too large for a tiny tummy to handle. For example, a half-cup of egg yolk can supply 20 percent of the calories a ten-month-old needs for the day. The same size portion of carrots will supply only 2 to 3 percent of the calories for the day, yet both foods will occupy the same space in your baby's stomach. Obviously the eggs are much more nourishing.

Besides calories, protein is extremely important. Protein from animal sources is called *complete protein*, because it contains the correct balance of amino acids needed by the body to maintain and build muscles. The same balance of complete proteins can be obtained by combining beans and grains; beans, nuts and seeds, or milk and grains. But these combinations must be planned carefully to ensure that your baby gets the protein he needs.

NUTRIENTS THAT MIGHT BE HARD TO GET ON A VEGETARIAN DIET

vitamin B$_{12}$	vitamin D
iron	protein
calcium	calories
folic acid	

It's not my intention to "bad-mouth" a vegetarian diet. A vegetarian diet can be a positive contribution to a healthy life. But a very restrictive vegetarian regime must be planned with great care for babies or adults. Don't be cavalier.

For help in planning a vegetarian diet, consult a registered dietitian by looking in the yellow pages under Nutritionists. See the appendix for additional resources on planning a vegetarian diet.

CHOLESTEROL

In the mid 1980s, interest in lowering blood cholesterol levels to prevent or reduce heart disease exploded. Physicians now routinely test blood cholesterol levels in adults, and people have been known to compare cholesterol results as if they were golf scores. In adults, cholesterol and other fats can build up in blood and block circulation, resulting in a stroke or heart attack. What people often don't realize, however, is that *cholesterol is essential to life*. It plays a role in the strengthening of cell membranes, protects nerve fibers and builds essential hormones. For these reasons you should never put your baby on a low-cholesterol diet. In fact, getting adequate amounts of cholesterol in infancy might protect your baby as she grows into an adult. Breast milk, the ideal baby food, has more cholesterol in it than cow's milk or formula. Mother Nature may have designed breast milk to be high in cholesterol because baby needs this fat and also because consumption at this early stage may teach the body to handle cholesterol in a healthy way.

Cholesterol is found in all animal foods, including meat, fish, poultry, cheese or milk and butter, and, of course, everyone knows that eggs have it. Any food that grows on a tree or is harvested from the ground—

wheat, vegetables—does not contain cholesterol.

If your family is on a low-cholesterol diet, that doesn't mean your baby can't enjoy the same wholesome foods you do. Fish, oat meal, lean beef, skinless poultry and margarine instead of butter are all fine for baby. However, because dairy foods such as milk and cheeses often make up a large portion of a baby's and a toddler's diet and provide the fat necessary for healthy growth, low-fat dairy products are not advised until after age two.

WHEN SHOULD YOU WORRY ABOUT CHOLESTEROL?

If an immediate family member such as Mom, Dad, Grandma or Grandpa has a high cholesterol level or has had a heart attack before age fifty, then the American Heart Association and the American Academy of Pediatrics say that a cholesterol test can be done as early as your baby's second birthday. But it is certainly not necessary to test all two-year-olds for cholesterol blood levels!

To test for cholesterol, your pediatrician will most likely measure total cholesterol first and, if warranted, follow up with a test for what is known as "good" HDL cholesterol and "bad" LDL cholesterol. Often these tests are done twice for accuracy. If a problem is found, the first line of defense is a healthy and delicious low-cholesterol diet. Ask your doctor for a referral to a registered dietitian—a nutritionist who can give you accurate, in-depth advice on living on a low-cholesterol diet that will be good for the whole family.

VITAMINS

If, after your baby is off formula or breast milk, you ask your pediatrician about the use of multivitamins, he or she will probably tell you to skip them. The American Academy of Pediatrics believes that the need for vitamin and mineral supplements does not exist in healthy children who eat well. This opinion is probably valid, but it is of little comfort to many parents of "fussy" eaters.

It's only natural to be concerned about a baby's or a toddler's nutrition, and to see vitamin supplements as "insurance." I think the medical community is opposed to the use of supplements because of their frequent misuse and their potential for toxicity. "After all," many adults reason, "what's the harm in a few extra vitamins? If a little is good, a lot must be better." This reasoning can truly be dangerous to a young child, whose small body is designed to handle nutrients only in small doses. Nature endows food with manageable amounts of many vitamins and minerals, but if nutrients are supplied by artificial means, via vitamin pills or liquid, the doses can far exceed what Mother Nature intended. Unless a child is fed large amounts of a particular food every day, such as vitamin A–rich carrot juice, it's nearly impossible to consume toxic levels of nutrients from food alone. It's easy if they're packed into vitamin supplements, however, especially if they're used imprudently.

Individual vitamins are rarely prescribed for children. The exceptions may be vitamin K at birth to prevent hemorrhagic disease, vitamin E to prevent a special type of anemia and the mineral iron or fluoride (see opposite). Doctors also often prescribe vitamin D for babies who are exclusively breast-fed.

So what are you to do about vitamins? The American Academy of Pediatrics says there is no need for a supplement, but you know you won't overuse them and you're worried about your little picky eater. Let common good sense be your guide. If you are providing your child with a balanced diet and he is growing well, he's probably eating enough, even if it doesn't look like it. If you still think he needs a supplement, then select one wisely. Ask your doctor to recommend a multivitamin and mineral supplement that does not exceed the RDA. Do *not* give single-nutrient supplements, as the chance for toxicity increases tremendously.

The vitamin and mineral supplements targeted for children under age four are monitored by FDA regulations to minimize misuse. The upper limits of individual nutrients in these are 100 to 150 percent of the RDA. The liquid drops for infants include vitamins A, C and D with or without iron. Vitamin E, thiamine, riboflavin, niacin and B_6 may or may not be included. The chewable tablets for toddlers contain all the nutrients as in the liquid form but may also contain folic acid and B_{12}.

Please remember that giving your child a vitamin or mineral supplement does not allow you to relax your guard against poor eating habits. There are almost thirty nutrients recognized by the National Academy of Sciences as being necessary for maintaining good health, and there are *no* supplements that supply all these vitamins and minerals in the recommended amounts. Supplements also do not provide calories, protein, fiber or trace elements. So while a supplement may give you some peace of mind and may help make up for a couple of unbalanced meals, it does not supply all your child's nutrient needs. Only food can do that.

So if you want a supplement, choose one that has both vitamins and minerals and

RECOMMENDED DIETARY ALLOWANCES

Nutrient	0–6 months	6–12 months	12–36 months
Protein grams	13	14	16
Vitamin A mcg	375	375	400
Vitamin D mcg	7.5	10	10
Vitamin E mg	3	4	6
Vitamin K mcg	5	10	15
Vitamin C mg	30	35	40
Thiamine mg	.3	.4	.7
Riboflavin mg	.4	.5	.8
Niacin mg	5	6	9
Vitamin B_6 mg	.3	.6	1
Folate mcg	25	35	50
Vitamin B_{12} mcg	.3	.5	.7
Calcium mg	400	600	800
Phosphorus mg	300	500	800
Magnesium mg	40	60	80
Iron mg	6	10	10
Zinc mg	5	5	10
Iodine mcg	40	50	70
Selenium mcg	10	15	20

From the tenth edition of the Recommended Dietary Allowances, National Research Council, 1989.

does not exceed the RDA. Then keep offering good food. Food tastes better than vitamins, and it's the only way to ensure the best nutrition for your child.

FLUORIDE

The one mineral you will find your doctor recommending enthusiastically is fluoride.

ESTIMATED SAFE AND ADEQUATE DAILY DIETARY LEVELS

Nutrient	0–6 months	6–12 months	12–36 months
Biotin mcg	10	15	20
Pantothenic acid mg	2	3	3
Copper mg	.4–.6	.6–.7	.7–1
Manganese mg	.3–.6	.6–1	1–1.5
Fluoride mg	.1–.5	.2–1	.5–1.5
Chromium mcg	10–40	20–60	20–80
Molybdenum mcg	15–30	20–40	25–50

From the tenth edition of the Recommended Dietary Allowances, National Research Council, 1989.

Ever since it was discovered that people who lived in areas with water that contained fluoride naturally had a dramatically lower rate of cavities, fluoride has been recommended as the main defense against tooth decay. Fluoride actually becomes part of the developing tooth and fortifies it, making it stronger to fight off cavity development. It may also help make bones stronger. Now many municipal water supplies are fluoridated, but if you do not live in an area that has fluoridated water, your pediatrician will recommend a fluoride supplement. Fluoride is recommended from shortly after birth up to the teen years, when the final permanent teeth all push through. Only your pediatrician can decide on the right dose. The decision is based on age and weight. The best time to take a fluoride supplement is on an empty stomach, say, at bedtime, because milk and some calcium-rich foods can interfere with its absorption.

If you obtain water from a well, you will have to test a sample to find out if your water contains fluoride. For a list of recommended water testers, see the water entry in the appendix. You shouldn't have too much or too little fluoride. However, if your baby is a big water drinker and you live in an area with fluoridated water, you don't have to worry about ingesting too much. Fluoride is added to the public water supply in tiny amounts

—one part fluoride to one million parts of water.

Though the benefits of fluoride have been known since the 1960s, there are still some individuals and groups who fear its use. Fluoride has been said to cause cancer and heart disease. These claims are erroneous. All the major health organizations support its use. If you still have concerns, discuss them with your pediatrician or write to the American Dental Association.

SMILE

Since we're on the subject of teeth, let's mention some common-sense steps to keep your baby's mouth and teeth in good health. It's so exciting when a baby gets her first tooth, and a good diet of milk, grains, proteins and vegetables will ensure that all the teeth she grows will be strong and healthy. But what and how she eats and drinks can help those teeth stay that way. Here are the five rules for healthy teeth:

1. Don't let your baby fall asleep at naptime or bedtime sucking on a bottle of juice, milk or formula. Your baby could develop "nursing bottle syndrome." This occurs when the upper front teeth are decayed by the liquid that bathes them while she sleeps.

2. If you want to give your little one sweet treats, give them at mealtimes, when saliva flow is greatest. It can help to "wash" the teeth.

3. Constant nibbling of sticky foods is more likely to cause cavities than an occasional sweet snack. There's nothing wrong with an occasional treat, but if you value healthy teeth, don't give your child constant access to sweets.

4. As soon as your child has several teeth, get into the habit of brushing or wiping teeth after meals. Pick a soft brush and, if your child likes the taste (many do!), use toothpaste.

5. *The first professional dental visit should be planned by age three.*

PESTICIDES: THE INVISIBLE FOE

The use of chemicals that cannot be seen but have the potential to harm our babies is a very scary problem. It was the 1989 Alar crisis that brought the whole issue of food safety out from the FDA offices and into the kitchen and grocery store.

Until recently, many people saw Alar, if they knew about it at all, as a harmless chemical that was sprayed on apple trees to

PESTICIDES IN PRODUCE

The pesticide residue in the apple you eat with lunch today or the carrot you cook tonight depends, among other things, on: the type, number and amount of pesticides applied; where and by whom the fruit or vegetable was grown; weather conditions, and the time it spent in storage; how well you've washed it; and whether you've peeled or cooked it.

With all these factors, it's just about impossible to know what's in *your* apple or carrot. Nonetheless, we have reviewed FDA and EPA data on residues of potential cancer-causing pesticides and have come up with the following recommendations on what to do—short of buying all organic produce—to minimize your risk. (While cancer isn't the only risk from pesticides in food, it's probably the major one.)

Eat as Usual	Wash	Wash Thoroughly	Special Handling
bananas	cabbage [1]	cauliflower	apples [O,P]
corn	cucumbers [2]	cherries	broccoli [O,S]
grapefruit	eggplant	grapes	carrots [3]
melons	peppers	green beans	celery [T]
oranges [4]	tomatoes	lettuce	peaches [O,P]
		potatoes	pears [O,P]
		strawberries	spinach [O,S]

[1] discard outer leaves
[2] peel, if waxed
[3] peel
[4] don't bite into peel; for grated peel, buy organic or wash thoroughly
[O] buy organic or IPM, if possible. IPM stands for Integrated Pest Management. It indicates food grown with a minimum of pesticides used.
[P] peel, if your diet is rich in fiber
[S] cut or chop, place in a bowl of water with a drop of liquid dishwashing detergent, agitate, then rinse thoroughly
[T] NRDC recommends trimming the leaves and top

keep the fruit on the tree and to keep it red during harvest and storage.

The problem started in 1985, when the United States Environmental Protection Agency found that in animal studies, Alar, the trade name for the chemical daminozide, broke down when it was heated into a chemical called UDMH. UDMH is also the chemical that is formed when apples treated with Alar are cooked to make sauce or juice, and it was found to be a cause of cancer. The Environmental Protection Agency proposed a ban on the use of Alar, but because the evidence on its link with cancer was said to be flawed, the ban didn't go into effect.

Meanwhile, many apple growers responded to the public's concern over Alar and stopped using it after the first alarm was sounded in 1985. Since then, the EPA has conducted additional studies that have found UDMH to be a substantial cancer risk. Most alarming is the fact that children are particularly vulnerable since they consume more apple juice and applesauce than adults do.

A study conducted by Consumers Union and published in the May 1989 *Consumer Reports* found that the presence of Alar in apple products was abundant. *CR* bought thirty-one apple juices, seven baby-food apple juices and twenty samples of raw apples. Eleven of the twenty red-apple samples had measurable levels of Alar, as did seven of the thirty-one apple juices tested. Most infant juice is made by one of three companies—Gerber, Beech-Nut and Heinz. The Consumers Union study found Gerber and Beech-Nut had no detectable levels of Alar while Heinz did contain some, though at a level well below the amounts found in adult juices.

The public outcry on this issue surprised everyone. As a result, Alar has been banned in this country and its use is allowed only in foreign markets. Consumer groups still say this is not enough: Foreign apples could make their way into our food supply. Since Alar is a potential carcinogen, why should babies in other countries go unprotected from the potential risks of this chemical?

Although the use of Alar has been stopped in the United States, until all the stored apples and apple concentrate have been used up, this substance will still be in some apple products. To avoid Alar, feed your baby only infant apple juice—evidently the baby-food companies do a better job of keeping the chemical out of their products. And instead of buying applesauce, make your own from fresh apples that have not been treated with Alar, or buy the kind made for infants.

Apples are by no means the only product that carries chemicals; almost all our produce, meat, poultry and even bread and grain contain some additives or pesticides. To reduce pesticide risk you can:

- Avoid "perfect" fruits and vegetables— more blemishes and flaws on produce may indicate the use of fewer chemicals.
- Buy local. Imported fruits and vegetables contain more pesticide residues.
- Wash your produce. Submerge it in water with a few drops of dishwashing detergent, then drain and rinse. Rinse very well. Soap residue could cause diarrhea.
- Peel waxed produce—the wax may be mixed with a fungicide. Thin coats of wax are frequently applied to apples, bell peppers, citrus fruits, eggplants, peaches, squash, sweet potatoes and tomatoes.

According to an article in *Nutrition Action*, published by Center for Science in the Public Interest (April 1989), beans, peas, sugar and oils have the lowest pesticide levels. Meat, fish, poultry, butter and lard contain the highest levels. These animal foods have higher pesticide residues because they naturally contain more fat than do plant foods such as beans and peas. So cut your and baby's risk of pesticide ingestion by trimming all extra fat off meat, and don't eat poultry skins, either.

For more information, see appendix.

PART 2

LET'S GET

COOKING

5

A KITCHEN PRIMER

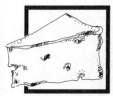

Part One is about when and how to start your baby on food. Now here is the hands-on information—what to cook in the microwave, and how. Cooking in a microwave is quite different from conventional cooking methods. To give you some understanding of how it works, here are some guidelines for successful cooking:

- *Foods with a high fat content cook the fastest. This means beef, lamb, pork, chicken, butter, whole milk or cheese recipes cook faster than vegetables or fruits.*
- *The temperature, not just the amount, of liquids used in recipes makes a difference.*

EASY OVEN CONVERSION

Power

Microwave ovens do not have standardized terms to describe temperature levels. Your oven will have either numbers, words or percentages to indicate the power level needed. Here is a simple conversion table:

100 percent = full power = level 10
50 percent = medium power = level 5

Cooking temperatures in this book will be referred to in percentages.

Cooking Times

The recipes in this book were all prepared in my 700-watt oven. Here's how you convert cooking times for different-sized ovens: Each time you use a particular recipe, note the cooking time variation and write it down in the cookbook. Next time you make the recipe, you won't need to think about it and you'll be making perfectly cooked food without having to refer back to this chart.

For a 500-watt oven: Add 40 seconds for each minute of my cooking time.
For a 600-watt oven: Add 20 seconds for each minute of my cooking time.
For a 650-watt oven: Cooking times are almost the same as in a 700-watt oven.
    Use my cooking times exactly.

Oven Size

Don't know your oven size? To test it, fill a dish with 1 cup of water. Cook at full power until it boils. If it boils in under 3 minutes, it is a 650- or 700-watt oven. If it takes longer, yours is a 500- or 600-watt oven.

A recipe using 1 cup of cold milk will take significantly longer than if that milk was at room temperature. The same holds for the temperature of water, broth or juices used in recipes. If you have trouble with the liquid boiling over in a recipe, you're using a bowl that's too small.

Oven size makes a difference. All the recipes in this book are written for a 700-watt oven. If your oven is smaller, it's easy to adjust cooking times. A 650- and a 700-watt oven have cooking times so similar, they can be considered identical, but the 400-, 500- or 600-watt models will need to have the recipe cooking times increased. (See the box opposite.)

PURÉEING

When you first start to cook for baby, most of the foods will need to be puréed. This conjures up visions of messy equipment and frustration, which is why so many mothers resort to jarred foods. But puréeing is simple. You just need the right proportion of liquid to solid to get good results. The age of your baby will determine the amounts: The smaller the baby, the more liquid you'll use. You don't need to buy any fancy equipment. Household appliances you already have, such as a food mill, food processor or blender, can all do the job. The grinders made specifically for baby foods are nice, too, because they are designed to purée small portions. Puréeing small servings in a blender can be frustrating because food gets stuck under the blade and you must keep scraping it out. Some foods that are stringy or tough will need to be strained after puréeing. This will be necessary only when your child is very young, until about six to eight months. Meats and chicken are the most difficult to strain. Macaroni is a little tough, too, but fruits and vegetables purée and strain beautifully.

TO STRAIN

Use a metal food strainer and push the food through the screen mesh with a rubber spatula. Any large or gritty pieces will be caught in the strainer, leaving a smooth purée for baby. Strainers are made of metal, so make sure that yours is not rusted and that the wires are firm and won't break off.

FROZEN FEASTS

One secret to easy baby meals is freezing. There's nothing quicker than taking a frozen homemade baby meal out of the freezer and popping it in the microwave for reheating. With few exceptions, the recipes in this book can be successfully frozen. Make portions large enough to be served at two meals, so that you can serve one half today and freeze the other half for another time. Try to use meals within two months to ensure that the food is still of the best quality. (Some foods held too long in the freezer can have a change in taste and texture.)

FIVE STEPS TO SUCCESSFUL FREEZING

1. If you plan to freeze a recipe, do so as soon as the dish has cooled. Don't let it sit around in the refrigerator for a few days before freezing.
2. Do not put foods into the freezer hot. It makes your freezer work too hard and causes ice crystals to form. Let it reach room temperature first.
3. Use the right size container and allow about ½ to 1 inch of air space between the food and the cover for expansion. Make sure the lid or cover you use fits securely.
4. Label everything. Include the name of the dish and the date it went into the freezer.
5. Use food within six to eight weeks.

If you want to freeze a lot of dinners for your baby, there are a number of containers and methods I can recommend. For infant-sized portions, put puréed food into ice cube trays, freeze, then pop out when frozen and keep stored in a plastic bag. You can use more or less of the cubes, depending on your baby's appetite. For larger portions, line small bowls with a plastic bag and pour in the mixture. When it's hard, remove it from the bowl and close the plastic bag. Or, line a muffin pan with paper muffin cups, and add mixture to be frozen. When frozen solid, remove from the freezer, let sit at room temperature for one minute, then plop out of the muffin tin and store in a plastic bag. Using a paper liner makes it easier to get the food out of the pan and into the bag. Just remember to remove the liner before heating and serving. Another method I've used successfully is to buy yogurt that's sold in the heavy, reusable plastic one-cup and four-cup containers. You'll be ecological *and* economical with this method. And finally, you can freeze in paper cups, and when the food is hard, transfer it, still in the cup, to a plastic bag. I do this when making broth. I make a large portion of broth in the microwave, then freeze eight-ounce portions in paper cups. I have just the right amount of broth to make flavorful rice or to use in baby-sized stews.

When freezing, keep these potential trouble spots in mind:

- Freezing can dry out food, so you may have to add some liquid, such as milk, juice or broth, when you reheat it.
- Potatoes often get mushy after freezing. Babies usually don't mind this but moms might think it looks funny. Try it anyway. See what *your* baby thinks.
- If you know you're cooking a dish only for freezing, you can slightly undercook vegetables and grains, knowing that they will get cooked again during reheating.

One of the real treasures of the microwave is its ability to thaw frozen foods, especially leftovers, rapidly. Many of us discovered this before we had children, but it's never more valuable than when we're feeding hungry little mouths besides our own. Check the chart above for temperatures and times, cook the food for the recommended period, then stir and cook longer if you need to. Smaller ovens may take longer to defrost. As I mentioned earlier, it never hurts to add a bit of extra liquid. If meats were undercooked, it's important to get them hot again; meat and poultry need to reach a temperature of 170 and 185 degrees, respectively. Keep in mind, too, that when you're using the microwave for defrosting, you need to use microwave-safe containers. That means no metal, and if you're defrosting

DEFROSTING AND REHEATING TIMES		
Size	**Time**	**Power**
½-cup portions	2½ minutes	medium
1-cup portions	4 minutes	medium

foods wrapped in plastic, remove the food from the plastic bag and place it in a microwave-safe dish first. Some experts suggest that the kind of plastic used to make plastic bags and plastic wrap can transfer chemicals to our food, so when you're defrosting, I recommend simply transferring the foods to microwave-safe dishes before reheating. The easiest way to get frozen food out of a plastic bag is simply to run it under hot water.

6

MY TOP ONE HUNDRED

When you first start to feed your baby, you will be cooking only single-ingredient foods. On the pages that follow I have developed a nutrition and cooking profile of the foods parents serve most frequently as well as the foods I'm asked about most often as a nutritionist. You will see that I have arranged this section alphabetically and included cooking and preparation information as well as important nutrition and storage suggestions. Use this as a quick reference. For example, if you want to cook an egg yolk for baby, look up Egg and read how to do it. You'll also read about important health and nutrition information connected with feeding eggs. Or, if you'd like to try your baby on tofu but don't know much about it, look it up and find out. If the whole family is eating oat bran cereal and you want to serve some to your toddler, then read about oat bran first.

For each food, I give serving instructions for two age groups: infants and toddlers. Based on their chewing ability, I define infants as babies four months to nine months. In this young age category, food must first be served as a very thin, watery gruel. It can then progress to purées, and, finally, to wet, lumpy mush. Somewhere around nine months, babies start to show teeth and develop what is called the pincer grasp, meaning they can pick up food between the thumb and forefinger. Then they can start even lumpier finger foods. By age nine months most children will be eating some foods with their fingers—pieces of cooked egg yolk, noodles and cooked soft vegetables and fruit. It is important to offer your child a variety of tastes and textures at this point so that his eating develops to match his potential. I always err on the side of caution. If you want to give your baby finger foods but fear choking, then chop up the food small enough so that it won't cause trouble.

In this index a toddler is a ten-month-old all the way up to a three-year-old. By ten months your baby can eat almost anything. The risk of allergies and food reactions has lessened, but the consistency of the food does matter. In the younger months your child will need food to be served in a soft form because most children have only a few teeth. As the months go by your child will be able to move from mashed food to finely chopped to bite-sized pieces.

Every child is different and develops the ability to eat independently at a different rate. Don't be a slave to my feeding recommendations; use them as a guide and work them to meet your baby's needs.

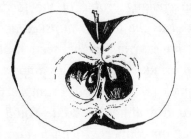

APPLES

Apples come in all colors, shapes and sizes, it seems. They can be eaten fresh or you can peel, core, cook and mash them for quick applesauce. Cooking time and taste will depend on the variety you buy. In the fall, when the season is at its peak, you may have twenty varieties to select from. Delicious and McIntosh make for better eating than cooking apples, and for baking, try a Cortland, Granny Smith or Rome Beauty.

To Prepare:
Peel, core and chop into even-size pieces. Put into a deep glass bowl, sprinkle with a little bit of water or juice and cover.

To Cook:
Cook 1 whole chopped apple for 1½ to 3 minutes, depending on size, at 100 percent power. Apple should be very soft. Remove cover carefully.

Infants:
Purée and strain. Simply mash when older. *Do not serve with skins at this early age.*

Toddlers:
Mash; add cinnamon and a pinch of sugar if the apple is very tart.

Storage:
Keep fresh ripe apples 2 to 4 weeks in a plastic bag and refrigerated. Once cooked, use in 2 days or freeze for 10 to 12 months.

Nutrition:
Apples have had a reputation for being very nutritious, but when compared to an orange or a banana they wouldn't win a nutrition contest. One apple contains only 4 milligrams of vitamin C (an orange would have 10 times that amount). Apples have only a small amount of vitamin A and the B vitamins. They do contain potassium and are a good fiber source, however.

Comments:
Avoid superglossy products: They probably get their shine from added wax. Until recently, some apples had been treated with Alar, a chemical linked with cancer (see pages 53–56). In May 1989 the International Apple Institute announced that United States apple growers would stop using the chemical Alar on crops. Any fresh apples bought after that date would be Alar-free.

APRICOTS

These are delicious fruits, but they have a short growing season and are available only briefly, usually in June or July. There is nothing quite as delicious as an apricot plucked straight from the tree! But for those of us who live far from an apricot grove, look in the store for fruits with deep color, avoiding those with a green tint. Dried apricots are more available and cook nicely.

FRESH APRICOTS

To Prepare:
Peel and pit 2 apricots, chop and put in a microwave-safe bowl.

To Cook:
Cook for 2 minutes, covered, at 100 percent.

DRIED APRICOTS

To Prepare:
Place ½ cup chopped dried apricots in a microwave-safe bowl, add ¼ cup water, cover.

To Cook:
Cook for 2 minutes at 100 percent, let rest 1 minute, then purée.

Infants:
Serve puréed at 6 to 8 months with enough water to thin it out.

Toddlers:
Serve the dried apricots cooked and puréed over rice or mixed with cereal. Fresh cooked apricots can be served just chopped or mashed. Uncooked dried apricots can be served to toddlers, if chopped into small pieces.

Storage:
Ripe, 2 to 3 days in refrigerator. Cooked and frozen, 10 to 12 months. Dried apricots can be kept 1 to 2 months in an airtight container in the refrigerator.

Nutrition:
Apricots are an excellent source of carotene, the precursor of vitamin A. They may protect against cancer.

ASPARAGUS

In the middle of winter, asparagus is an extravagant treat for little ones, but in season it's plentiful and wonderfully fresh. Tender cooked stalks can make a fun finger food for your toddler.

To Prepare:
Cut off the woody part of the stalk. You want to use only the tip and the closest tender part of the stem. Arrange in a flat layer in a microwave-safe dish. Add 1 tablespoon water.

To Cook:
Cook 5 stalks for 3 minutes, covered, at 100

percent. Rinse with cold water to cool and preserve color.

Infants:

The structure of the stalk makes straining hard to do, so hold off on this vegetable until baby can eat nonstrained foods. Try it puréed at about 8 months of age.

Toddlers:

Mash, chop or serve as a finger food.

Storage:

Keep refrigerated fresh for 4 to 6 days; cooked for 2 days; cooked and frozen for 8 to 10 months.

Nutrition:

Asparagus provides small amounts of protein and calcium, but it is a very good source of vitamin A and vitamin C, a good source of potassium and the B vitamins, and it even has a little iron.

Comments:

If after eating asparagus your baby or toddler has a funny-smelling urine, don't be alarmed. For centuries asparagus lovers have known this peculiar quirk of the vegetable. Apparently the amino acid known as methionine breaks down into an odorous compound that becomes the smelly but harmless culprit.

AVOCADO

When avocados are ripe, they are Mother Nature's contribution to convenience foods: They are available in single portions and can be eaten right out of the skin! Babies and toddlers love avocados.

To Prepare:

A ripe avocado needs little preparation. Just peel, remove the pit and mash with a fork. Add some applesauce, banana, juice or water to moisten and thin it out, if needed.

To Cook:

To "ripen" a hard avocado, slice it in half, remove the pit, put both halves facedown on a microwave-safe dish and cover. Cook 1 minute at 100 percent. Remove cover carefully. Rinse with cold water to stop cooking.

Infants:

Avocados may be too rich for first-time eaters, so hold off until age 8 months and then serve puréed or mashed.

Toddlers:

Serve ripe chunks or slices as a finger food (but watch out, kids love the squishy feel, so things could get messy). Or, serve mashed with a spoon.

Storage:

Keep at room temperature until ripe, then store in the refrigerator for up to 2 weeks.

Nutrition:

Very rich in potassium, a good source of vitamin C and vitamin A and very low in sodium. Very rich in vegetable fats—a 1-cup portion of avocado purée contains about 384 calories, 326 of which are from fat.

BACON

Bacon is too high in fat and sodium to appear regularly on your child's menu, but many kids regard it as a treat. Canadian bacon is leaner than sliced bacon and might be a better alternative, but it is quite high in sodium, too. Use both sparingly.

SLICED BACON

To Prepare:

Place 2 slices on 2 sheets of paper towel and cover with another sheet.

To Cook:

Cook at 100 percent for 2 minutes.

CANADIAN BACON

To Prepare:

Arrange 2 slices on a single paper towel.

To Cook:

Cook at 100 percent for 1 minute.

Infants:

Too salty. Don't serve it.

Toddlers:

Serve crisp bacon as a finger food or crumbled and mixed in with vegetables or stew. Canadian bacon must be chopped and treated the same as eating a piece of ham.

Storage:

Sliced bacon—eat within a week of "sell by" date. Once opened, use within 7 days. Can be frozen, wrapped in plastic, for 1 month. Canadian bacon—keeps 3 to 4 days in refrigerator if wrapped tightly. Can be frozen for 3 to 6 weeks.

Nutrition:

Two thin slices have 60 calories; about 12 of those calories are as protein and 45 calories are as fat. The same portion of Canadian bacon has only about 30 calories, 12 of them as protein, 18 as fat. Both are very high in sodium.

BANANAS

I don't think there's a baby who doesn't adore bananas, and because bananas make babies happy, they make mothers happy, too.

To Ripen:

Cook with peel on at 100 percent for 1 minute and allow to rest for 1 minute. Heating in this way may cause a black ring to form at the tip and tail of the banana. This method makes the banana softer, but the taste is not as good as when time does the ripening.

Infants:

Serve ripe bananas starting at 4 to 6 months. Purée or mash thoroughly with added water or allowed juice.

Toddlers:

Serve mashed or cut up as a finger food. To reduce the risk of choking, slice raw bananas lengthwise, not in short round pieces that can act as dangerous plugs if inhaled or swallowed whole.

Storage:

Keep at room temperature. If you refrigerate, the skin turns black, though the fruit is still good. Bananas can keep about a week, then they run the risk of overripening. Banana purée can be frozen up to 3 months if mixed with a little lemon juice.

Nutrition:

Most of a small banana's 81 calories come from high-energy carbohydrates. A banana has just a little bit of calcium, iron and vitamin C. It is a good natural source of potassium.

BARLEY

Barley makes a great alternative to rice. I use quick-cooking pearl barley. It's a little bland on its own, but it can be flavored by cooking it in juice or stock.

To Prepare:

Mix ¼ cup pearl barley with 1 cup liquid—water, broth or juice.

To Cook:

Cover, cook at 100 percent in a 4-cup microwave-safe dish for 3 minutes. Let barley rest, covered, for 10 minutes before serving. If it is still firm, cook again for 2 to 3 minutes, making sure there is enough liquid in the dish. If the barley has been in your cupboard for a while, you will probably need the extra cooking time. Drain if needed and purée with reserved liquid.

Infants:

Barley can be sampled as early as 4 to 6

months, but it is not iron-fortified like the commercial boxes of dry infant cereals.

Toddlers:

Serve with chopped fruit, vegetables or meat mixed in.

Storage:

Barley can keep for up to a year. Once cooked, use it within a day. Since it is easy to prepare, there is usually no need to freeze barley, but you could, in a plastic bag, if you wanted to.

Nutrition:

Barley contains a little iron, is a good potassium source and contains the B vitamins thiamine, riboflavin and niacin.

BEANS

Some beans cook beautifully in the microwave, others take quite a long time, but all are popular with kids.

FRESH GREEN OR YELLOW BEANS

A bean is easy to hold, and that alone might make it popular with your little one. Buy beans that are small and tender.

To Prepare:

Trim off tails and stems, remove strings if necessary. Chop into small pieces.

To Cook:

Place 1 cup beans in a 2-cup-sized microwave-safe bowl with a sprinkling of water. Cover and cook at 100 percent for 3 minutes. Let rest an additional 2 to 3 minutes, covered.

Infants:

Purée with added water.

Toddlers:

Beans don't mash very well, so if your little one isn't ready for chopped vegetables, give beans a quick spin in the blender to mash them up. Or, chop into small pieces for a finger food.

Storage:

Fresh beans can last 3 to 5 days. Once cooked, use within 2 or 3 days. Frozen, they can last for 10 to 12 months.

Nutrition:

Green beans contain 3 times the amount of vitamin A that yellow beans do. Both contain vitamin C and some of the B vitamins.

DRIED BEANS

(Lentils, chick-peas, black-eyed peas, kidney beans and navy beans)

Lentils and black-eyed peas cook easily in the microwave. Kidney beans, garbanzos (chick-peas) and navy beans take longer. The canned versions of these may be a quicker, easier alternative for you.

To Prepare:

Wash and presoak dried beans. To presoak, let beans sit in a bowl of water overnight or cook 1 cup dried beans with 3 cups water (to prevent boiling over, use a very large, 8-cup pot). Cover and cook at 100 percent for 10 minutes. Let stand 10 minutes. Stir and cook at 100 percent for 5 minutes, adding more water if it has all been absorbed. Let stand 1 hour.

To Cook:

For ½ cup drained, presoaked beans, cover and cook with 1 cup water or broth for 8 minutes at 100 percent. Let rest 15 minutes. If the beans are not tender, cook 5 minutes more and let rest, covered, 10 more minutes. Add ½ cup liquid before cooking if they appear dry.

Infants:

Hold off until 8 to 10 months of age, then serve puréed or mashed smooth, mixed with a little yogurt, milk or juice.

Toddlers:

Serve mashed or chopped.

Storage:

Dried beans can keep for a year. Cooked beans should be used in a day or two.

Nutrition:

One cup of beans provides about 13 grams of protein, but it is not of the same quality as animal protein. To make the protein in beans complete, they must be served with either rice or wheat, which have the amino acids beans lack.

Comments:

Cooking dried beans is time-consuming no matter what method you use. Canned beans are easy to use, but rinse them before serving. Rinsing removes the added sodium, but it does not wash away the important protein they contain.

BEEF

Beef can be cooked so many different ways that even the finickiest eater likes at least ten different beef dishes. Beef is easy to store for quick cooking, too: Shape fresh ground beef into 2-ounce balls and freeze on a dinner plate, then plop into a plastic bag. When a recipe calls for a small amount of ground meat, you'll have just the right size. Overcooking in the microwave can toughen beef, but adequate heat is needed to kill potentially harmful organisms. Never give a baby rare meat.

To Prepare:
Depending on the cut, trim fat, then cut into ¼-inch cubes.

To Cook:
For a 2-ounce piece, cook in ¼ cup water, broth or tomato juice for 2 minutes, covered. Must be steaming hot. Stir. Let rest 3 to 5 minutes.

GROUND BEEF

To Prepare:
Mix 2 ounces ground beef with ¼ cup water, broth or tomato juice, or shape 2 ounces ground beef into a small, thin patty.

To Cook:
Cook at 100 percent for 2 minutes. Cover the patty with a paper towel to prevent grease from splattering. Must be steaming hot. Stir. Let rest, covered, for 2 to 3 minutes to allow for complete cooking.

Infants:
Purée. Serve meat cooked in water or broth, not tomato juice. (Infants are too young to

digest tomatoes well.) Infants will prefer the beef cooked in liquid over the drier beef patty method.

Toddlers:
Serve beef finely chopped. All meat is chewy, so make sure it is served in a form that matches your child's chewing ability.

Storage:
Fresh beef can last up to 5 days if refrigerated at a cold temperature. Ground beef should be used within 1 day of purchase. All beef can be frozen for up to 10 to 12 months.

Nutrition:
Beef is an excellent source of protein and iron. "Prime" beef may cost more, but it is no more nutritious than the less expensive "choice" cuts.

Comments:
When fresh red meat turns brown, it does not mean it has spoiled; the browning occurs when beef is exposed to air. A change in color does mean it should be used soon, however.

Is hormone-treated beef safe to eat? According to the Food and Drug Administration, yes. In this country, 70 to 90 percent of all the cattle are treated with hormones to make them gain weight fast. Most studies have found that cattle treated with the correct dose of hormones pose no health risks to consumers and that the amount of residual hormone in the beef is very, very small.

The consumer group Center for Science in the Public Interest, however, has concerns that if hormones are not properly used, beef may contain levels that are above amounts proven to be safe. The only alternative to buying hormone-treated beef is to buy certified untreated beef. While the official word is that beef is very safe, this problem does underscore the importance of eating a wide variety of foods. That means alternating beef with other protein sources, such as lamb, poultry, beans and dairy products. Variety decreases the chance of ingesting something harmful from one particular food or food group.

BEETS

Preparing fresh beets in the microwave is so easy you'll want to serve them much more often than you probably do now.

To Prepare:
Cut off tops. Wash, then cover with water in a microwave-safe bowl.

To Cook:
Cook 2 beets, 2 inches in diameter, about 4 minutes at 100 percent. Once beets are cooked, run them under running cold water and slip off the tough skins with your fingers or trim with a knife.

Infants:
Purée with added cooking juice, if needed.

Toddlers:
Serve mashed or chopped. Beets can also be a finger food, but the bright red color makes eating very messy, so be careful.

Storage:
Fresh beets last 7 to 10 days, but remove the green leaves because they drain out needed moisture. Beet greens are tasty, too. Read about them under Greens. Cooked beets should be used within 3 days, or freeze for 2 to 4 months.

Nutrition:
Two cooked beets have about 32 calories.

They are often thought to be high in sodium, but a serving contains only 43 milligrams of sodium. They contain small amounts of many vitamins, including A and C, as well as the mineral potassium.

Comments:

Beets may be naturally high in nitrates, which can change to potentially harmful nitrites in baby's stomach. A sometimes lethal condition called methemoglobinemia could result from too many nitrites. A baby would probably need to eat enormous quantities of beets in order to get it, but to be on the safe side, serve beets only once a day.

BLUEBERRIES

Living near the Maine coast means that in August, delicious fresh blueberries will be on our table. These sweet berries can be served raw, but when gently cooked they make a superb syrup or sauce.

To Prepare:

Wash and pick over berries, removing any green berries, stems or stones.

To Cook:

Cook ½ cup berries with ¼ cup water (add 1 teaspoon sugar if tart, or cook in fruit juice instead of water). Cook, covered, at 100 percent for 3 minutes.

Infants:

Purée and strain to remove skins (for very young infants). Serve mixed with cereal or pour over yogurt or cooked rice.

Toddlers:

Fresh blueberries can be a fun finger food, or cook them and pour over fresh sliced bananas, pancakes (instead of syrup) or yogurt.

Storage:

Fresh blueberries should be used within 2 to 3 days. Frozen fresh in a rigid plastic container, they will keep for up to 12 months.

Nutrition:

Like all fruit, blueberries are naturally low in calories. They are a good source of vitamin C and a rich fiber source, too.

BRAN

Bran is the outer shell of wheat. It is removed when making white flour. Bran is an easy and inexpensive way for adults to get fiber, but adding bran to a young child's diet is not advised. Too much bran could cause digestive disturbances such as gas and cramping, and it may bind with important nutrients, making them unavailable to your baby. A baby should get fiber from whole foods, not bran.

BREAD

If you're looking for a good bread, don't bother trying to cook it in the microwave. Bread baking is not the microwave's strong point. Bread is a very good food for children, though, and I recommend the whole-grain breads even for young eaters. I think they taste better, and they contain healthy amounts of fiber, trace elements such as zinc and copper and are a good source of B vitamins. Most breads contain 70 to 75 calories per slice and 2 to 3 grams of protein.

A loaf of bread can last 2 to 4 days at room temperature, and twice as long in the refrigerator. If tiny mold spots appear, you can cut them off and the bread will be okay to serve, but finish it that day.

Serving Ideas:
Toast is a great finger food and a good wholesome snack, too. Instead of butter or jelly, spread toast with mashed bananas or cooked mashed peaches or pears.

BROCCOLI

At least one famous American hates broccoli, and for a long time I didn't serve broccoli to Sarah, either. I prepared it once before her first birthday and she didn't like it. Maybe the taste was too strong for her. Then, at about eighteen months, she tried it again and it turned out to be a favorite. I think she likes the bright green color and the fact that it looks like a little tree. Our President, meanwhile, still keeps it off his menu.

To Prepare:
Cut off and chop into even-sized pieces enough of the "flowers" to equal ½ cup. The flowers are more tender than the stalks and are more likely to be popular with young children.

To Cook:
Cover. Sprinkle with water. Cook 2 to 3 minutes at 100 percent until tender.

Infants:
Broccoli can be puréed with water, but it was never popular with my kids at this age.

Toddlers:

Serve chopped, or let your child eat it as a finger food sprinkled with a little lemon, butter or grated cheese.

Storage:

Fresh broccoli should be used within 5 days or the tops turn yellow, indicating a loss of nutrients. It can be frozen for 10 to 12 months.

Nutrition:

All of the broccoli plant is edible. In fact, the leaves contain more vitamin A than the stalks or flowers. Broccoli, along with cauliflower and Brussels sprouts, is a member of the cruciferous vegetable family, which is credited with fighting cancer.

BROTH

Many of my recipes can be made with broth instead of water. By making your own broth, you'll know it has no added salt or other additives (making a soup stock or broth on the stove top takes forever, but in the microwave it is easy).

To Cook:

Take 1 1-pound beef shin bone, lamb shank or poultry carcass, put in a 1- to 2-quart microwave-safe bowl, add a chopped onion, a bay leaf and enough water to cover. Cook at 100 percent for 15 minutes. Let sit for 30 minutes. Remove bone and seasoning. Yields about 3 cups. Store in 1-cup containers and freeze.

Tip:

The cooled broth can be poured into 8-ounce paper cups, frozen, then plopped into plastic bags and removed as needed.

BRUSSELS SPROUTS

Some kids love these "little cabbages" and others find them too strong in flavor. Offer them at least once to see how your kids like them.

To Prepare:

Remove loose leaves, trim bottoms, slice into quarters. Place in a single layer, sprinkle with water, cover.

To Cook:

Cook 3 sprouts 2 to 3 minutes at 100 percent.

Infants:

Many adults complain that Brussels sprouts make them feel gassy, so you may not want to risk the same problem with your little baby.

Toddlers:
Serve chopped or cook until very tender and mash. While still hot, sprinkle with a little cheese.

Storage:
Brussels sprouts will keep 3 to 5 days in the refrigerator and 10 to 12 months if frozen.

Nutrition:
Brussels sprouts are an excellent fiber source. They contain vitamin A, potassium and vitamin C.

BULGUR

This is a wheat berry that is steamed and then dried. It makes a nice alternative to rice. On its own it is a bit bland, but cooked in broth or served mixed with cooked fruit, it's delicious. Once cooked it triples in volume.

To Prepare:
Bring 2½ cups water to a boil by cooking it in your microwave for 2 to 4 minutes. Mix ½ cup bulgur into the hot water.

To Cook:
Cook for 1 minute at 100 percent. Cover and let steep in hot water for 25 minutes. Drain any excess liquid.

Infants:
Cooked bulgur is the size of a grain of rice. It will need to be puréed for first-time eaters. Serve after age 8 months.

Toddlers:
Serve in place of rice with a dab of butter, mixed with fruit or cooked meat.

Storage:
Bulgur should be used within a month if kept at room temperature. It will last much longer if kept in the refrigerator.

Nutrition:
Contains small amounts of riboflavin, niacin, potassium, calcium and iron.

CABBAGE

For some reason, cabbage is a vegetable parents may be reluctant to try on their kids, but some kids really do like it, so tell them the story of Peter Rabbit in Mr. MacGregor's cabbage patch and test cabbage at least once when they're old enough.

To Prepare:
Remove outside leaves if dry, cut a large wedge from the head and chop into bite-size pieces.

To Cook:
Cover and cook at 100 percent for 3 minutes for ½ cup. Leaves should be very tender.

Infants:
Forget it. I doubt your little one will like puréed cabbage.

Toddlers:
Some kids like cabbage, others don't. Try tossing cooked cabbage with butter or applesauce or sautée it with cooked potatoes.

Storage:
A head of cabbage lasts 1 to 2 weeks, but once it's sliced it starts to wilt and should be used quickly.

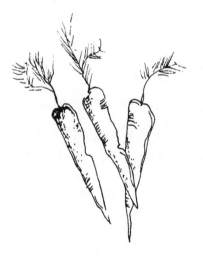

Nutrition:
Cabbage provides vitamin C, potassium and some vitamin A as well as small amounts of many other nutrients.

Comments:
Sauerkraut, popular with some adults, is salted, fermented cabbage, and is too high in sodium to be regularly served as a vegetable to small children.

CARROTS

Carrots are a fun vegetable for little children to grow in a garden. If you don't have a vegetable patch, bring a bunch of carrots home sometime with their green tops still on. When cooked until tender, carrots are always a favorite.

To Prepare:
Remove tops, and scrub or peel if the outside skin has a bitter taste. Cut into julienne strips or carrot coins, then chop. Sprinkle with water.

To Cook:
Cover and cook ½ cup for 3 minutes at 100 percent.

Infants:
Purée.

Toddlers:

Serve chopped or mashed.

Storage:

Trim off tops if present, to conserve moisture. Store refrigerated in plastic for 1 to 2 weeks. Can be frozen for 10 to 12 months.

Comments:

Do not serve carrots as a teething food. They can break off and plug tiny airways. Serve raw carrots in strips, grated or chopped. Some carrots are naturally rich in nitrates, which can be converted into nitrites, which are potentially toxic. For this reason, limit carrots to once a day. The problem is most likely to occur in the first six months of life.

Nutrition:

Carrots are one of the best sources of carotene, the precursor to vitamin A, a nutrient credited with being a cancer fighter. Carrot juice as a regular drink could provide a baby with too much vitamin A to handle as well as too many nitrates (see above).

CAULIFLOWER

This is one of my favorite fresh vegetables. A large head of cauliflower is more than two people can eat right away, so now that I

have children to cook for, I want them to like it, too.

To Prepare:

Chop the florets into small pieces equal to ½ cup.

To Cook:

Cook ½ cup with a sprinkling of water, covered, for 3 minutes at 100 percent.

Infants:

Purée with water or juice. It can cause a gassy stomach in adults and might do the same for baby if served in large quantities.

Toddlers:

Serve chopped, mashed or as a finger food. You can top hot cauliflower with a slice of mild cheese before serving.

Storage:

Fresh will last 4 to 7 days in the refrigerator; cooked, 2 to 3 days in the refrigerator; and frozen, up to 12 months.

Nutrition:

Good source of vitamin C.

CELERY

I used to buy celery only when I needed it in stews and soups, and I always found that I had most of the bunch left over afterward. Finally I discovered a recipe for cooked celery, although Emily was never a big fan. I include the following recipe, though, in case you have lots of celery and want to try it!

To Prepare:

Wash and peel with a vegetable peeler to remove strings, and chop.

To Cook:

Cook 1 cup chopped celery with 1 tablespoon water, covered, at 100 percent for 3 to 4 minutes.

Infants:

No.

NUTRITIONAL CONTENT OF SOME CHEESES

Cheese	Calories	Protein	Calcium	Sodium
Cheddar	113	7.1 gm	213 mg	198 mg
cottage	30	3.9 gm	27 mg	65 mg
cream	106	2.3 gm	18 mg	71 mg
Swiss	105	7.8 gm	262 mg	201 mg
American	105	6.6 gm	198 mg	322 mg

Nutrition data from USDA Handbook 456.

Toddlers:

Celery can be a tasty cooked vegetable, though it is often overlooked. Serve it cooked and chopped into bite-size pieces. Slice raw celery into thin slices to minimize the risk of choking.

Storage:

Can keep up to 2 weeks in the refrigerator. Celery is so plentiful, there really is no need to freeze it.

Nutrition:

Rich in fiber.

CHEESE

Cheese does not need to be cooked for babies, but you will use it in recipes and there are a lot of varieties to choose from. Those with the most protein and calcium and the least amount of sodium are the best bets. All cheese (except low-fat varieties) provides a lot of fat. The nutritional information at left is for a 1-ounce portion.

Storage:

Most hard cheese should be used within 4 to 8 weeks. I keep a plastic lidded container in my refrigerator that I store all our cheese in. It keeps it fresh, I can find it in a hurry, and

I have no "dry" spots. Ricotta, cream cheese and cottage cheese all have "sell by" dates and should be used by the date stated.

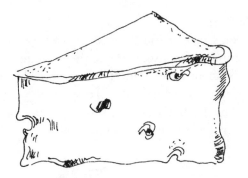

CHICKEN
. . . .

Parents put chicken on their own menu because it is relatively low in fat and calories and can be prepared in so many ways, from Southern fried to French coq au vin. Chicken is a wonderful, easy food for little ones, too—packed with protein and easy to prepare in the microwave for any age baby or child.

To Prepare:
Remove skin, but leave meat on the bone because the bone enhances flavor and is easier to remove after it is cooked.

To Cook:
Cook ½ chicken breast with 1 tablespoon water for 3 minutes at 100 percent. Cook 1 leg with thigh with 1 tablespoon water for 5 minutes at 100 percent. Chicken must always be cooked until it is steaming hot, then let rest, covered, for 3 to 5 minutes so that it is heated all the way through.

Infants:
Purée with broth or water and strain.

Toddlers:
Chop; can be eaten as a finger food.

Storage:
Use uncooked chicken within 24 hours; cooked should be eaten in 2 days. Frozen, cooked chicken should be used within a month. Well-wrapped raw chicken can be frozen up to 9 months.

Nutrition:
Chicken is a good protein source, and the dark meat contains more iron than the light.

Comments:
It is very important that chicken be completely cooked to kill any salmonella that may be present.

CHOCOLATE
. . . .

Despite the claims of grown-up "chocaholics," chocolate is not a member of any of the food groups, but served at appropriate times it can be a real treat. Infants have no need for chocolate, and served before 8 or 9 months it could cause an allergic reaction.

HOT CHOCOLATE

Made the old-fashioned way, with whole milk, this can be a nutritious drink. Serve this to children who are drinking out of a cup as a special treat. Mix 1 tablespoon pre-sweetened cocoa with 1 cup milk. Cook at 100 percent for 1 minute. Let cool. Or, mix 1 teaspoon unsweetened cocoa with 2 teaspoons sugar and 1 cup milk. Cook 1 minute. To guarantee smoothness, mix the sugar, cocoa and ¼ cup of the milk and heat it for 15 seconds on high, then stir in remaining milk and finish cooking another 45 seconds. Let cool.

Nutrition:

Most of the calories in chocolate come from fat. It contains very small amounts of a few vitamins and minerals, but nothing significant. It does contain some caffeine.

CORN

Sweet fresh corn is a favorite in our house, and cooking whole ears in the microwave is easy and delicious.

WHOLE CORN

To Prepare:

Leave husk and silk intact.

To Cook:

Cook 1 ear 2 minutes at 100 percent (about 6 minutes for a smaller oven). Let stand in husk about 2 to 3 minutes. Corn should feel hot all over when done. To speed serving, plunge fresh cooked ears of corn in cold water to cool them off faster.

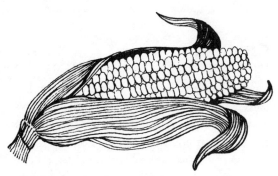

CORN KERNELS

To Prepare:

Remove husk and silk, and cut off kernels by running a sharp knife down the cob. Put in a microwave-safe dish with 1 tablespoon water, cover and cook at 100 percent for 4 minutes.

Infants:

No.

Toddlers:
Serve corn after 8 months of age, chopped, creamed or on the cob.

Storage:
Fresh corn should be used within 1 day. The sugar in corn quickly turns from sweet to starchy with age. Corn can be frozen after cooking either as kernels or whole.

Nutrition:
Corn is very rich in fiber.

CORNMEAL (ALSO CALLED POLENTA)

Kids love this simple, mild-tasting meal. It is a bit bland on its own, but mixed with cheese, cooked with milk, topped with a tomato sauce or made into a pudding, it is very good. It can also be eaten as a hot breakfast cereal with milk and fruit.

To Prepare:
Mix ¼ cup cornmeal with 1 cup water or ½ cup water and ½ cup milk when baby is old enough to have cow's milk.

To Cook:
Cook in a 4-cup bowl, uncovered, for 3 minutes. Stir and mash lumps. Watch out: The dish will probably be quite hot. Let rest, covered, 2 minutes, to complete cooking, and allow to cool before serving.

Infants:
Because this is made from corn, hold off until 8 months of age.

Toddlers:
Serve as is or top with a little butter or cheese, or mix in some applesauce or cooked fruit.

Storage:
Cornmeal can last 6 to 12 months when stored in a cool, dark place. Older cornmeal may require slightly longer cooking times.

Nutrition:
Cornmeal is a good source of niacin, iron, thiamine and riboflavin.

COUSCOUS

Instant couscous is available in most supermarkets. It is refined, which means it has lost much of the fiber and some of the vitamins, but it is a nice alternative to rice and very easy to prepare.

To Prepare:
Heat 1 cup water for 2 minutes at 100 percent, then add ½ cup couscous.

To Cook:
Cook couscous 1 minute at 100 percent. Stir, cover, let rest 5 minutes.

Infants:
Serve plain as is after age 8 months.

Toddlers:
Serve in place of rice.

Storage:
Keep in a cool dark place. Use within 6 months.

Nutrition:
Contains a few B vitamins and is low in fat and sodium.

CRACKERS

By age 12 months, your baby can eat store-bought crackers, and most mothers turn to them as a quick snack. Many crackers are loaded with salt and fat, though, so take some time to choose a healthy product carefully. "Wheat" does not always mean whole wheat, and "unsalted" may mean there is no salt on the surface but it may be cooked right into the cracker. Added fat is another special problem. Nabisco's Ritz crackers and Cheese Tid-Bits, Keebler's Club and Town House crackers, as well as Pepperidge Farm's Goldfish crackers, get 40 to 50 percent of their calories from fat. You may wonder why I worry about fat in crackers since I say children under age 2 don't need to be on low-fat diets. Children do need fat, but they should get it from the foods that contain it naturally, such as meat and dairy products. Fat added to naturally low-fat foods such as wheat is simply unnecessary and may contribute to a taste for high-fat foods in adulthood.

The following is a list of recommended crackers I adapted from the *Nutrition Action Health Letter.* These crackers are the best bet for babies, and healthy for the rest of the family, too:
Wasa Crispbread, hearty rye
Wasa Crispbread, lite rye
Venus salt-free bran or corn
Ryvita rye crisp bread
Ryvita sesame rye crisp bread
Norseland Original Rye Finn Crisp

Always be careful when serving crisp crackers to little eaters. You may have to break them into small pieces so that children can chew or gum them easily.

If you're wondering if graham crackers or saltines are okay for baby, rest easy. Two graham crackers have about 60 calories, only 13 of which are from fat, and they are low in sodium. Saltines are also low in fat, but they contain 40 milligrams of sodium in

1 cracker. That is not much if your baby eats just 1 cracker, but if your child develops a taste for them and eats a lot, the sodium could be significant.

CRANBERRIES

These berries are so pretty, but without a lot of sugar they taste terrible. I cook them in juice instead of sugar. Even cooked in sweet juice they have a tart taste. Try serving mixed with applesauce or yogurt.

To Prepare:
Wash cranberries. Chop coarsely and mix ¾ cup with ⅓ cup fruit juice or ⅓ cup fruit-juice concentrate.

To Cook:
Cook 5 minutes, uncovered, at 100 percent. Then cover and let rest 2 minutes.

Infants:
Not recommended because they are hard to purée.

Toddlers:
Serve for dessert.

Storage:
Peak availability is in the fall. Fresh berries can last up to 1 month and frozen fresh for 12 months.

Nutrition:
Fresh cranberries contain fiber and vitamin C. Cranberry-juice cocktail contains only 27 percent cranberry juice. The remaining ingredients are water, high fructose and added vitamin C. Canned cranberry sauce is high in calories, and much of the vitamin C is destroyed in the canning process.

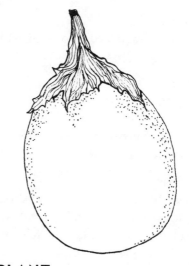

EGGPLANT

Until I started experimenting with recipes for my children, eggplant was not a regular on my grocery list. Now it is. The cooking instructions below are good, but when your child is a little older, try the Moussaka recipe (see page 166). It's delicious, and grown-ups will want to have some, too!

To Cook:

Leave the eggplant whole, prick the skin several times to release steam and cook 10 to 12 minutes at 100 percent. When done it should feel hot and soft.

Infants:

Remove the seeds, serve only the pulp, puréed with a little juice or water.

Toddlers:

Scoop out the cooked pulp, mash with a fork or chop.

Storage:

Fresh eggplant can keep 3 to 4 days; once cooked, use it within 2 days. It can be cooked and frozen as a purée (with a teaspoon of lemon juice) for up to 6 months.

Nutrition:

Cooked eggplant is no dietary powerhouse. It is low in calories and a good source of fiber, but vitamins and minerals are available only in small amounts.

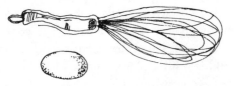

EGGS

Eggs come packed by Mother Nature in neat little one-serving containers, and are a versatile food for babies and children. The microwave cooks them beautifully, and they can be served hot or cold. Ever since cholesterol has become a household word, egg consumption has been on the downslide, but eggs deserve to be a part of your child's diet. At this young age she needs cholesterol and fat for proper brain development and growth. (Read about cholesterol in Chapter 4.)

To Cook:

Read about cooking eggs in Chapter 11.

Infants:

To start, serve only the yolk, but wait until baby is at least 8 months old. Hold off on egg white until at least 10 months, because children are more likely to be allergic to the protein-rich white than the yolk. Remove the yolk from the cooked egg and serve mashed.

Toddlers:

Serve cut up, or chop hard-cooked eggs as a finger food.

Storage:

Clean, unbroken eggs can be refrigerated in their original container, which keeps them fresher, for up to 1 month. Hard-cooked eggs in the shell can last 3 weeks.

Nutrition:
One egg supplies more protein than 1 ounce of meat and is a good source of vitamin A.

Comments:
The color of the eggshell does not affect the nutritional value or taste of the egg, but the grading system can be an indicator of taste. Grade AA are the freshest eggs, followed by Grade A and finally Grade B. In general, the fresher the egg, the better the flavor, but all grades share the same nutrition profile.

Even Grade AA uncracked eggs have been found to be infected with salmonella, so all eggs must be thoroughly cooked. Never serve your child a soft-boiled egg.

FIGS

Fresh figs, when you can get them, are a nice way to add variety to your baby's menu. Dried figs can be cut up and eaten like raisins, and older babies and toddlers enjoy their naturally sweet taste and chewy texture.

FRESH FIGS

To Cook:
If fully ripe, a fig needs no cooking. To poach or stew, peel, slice, cover with water and cook for 2 minutes at 100 percent.

Infants:
Little babies won't like the texture of the tiny fig seeds. Since these are hard to remove, hold off serving figs until older.

Toddlers:
Chop or mash or serve as a finger food in raw chunks.

DRIED FIGS

These can be eaten like raisins, but chop them up for young eaters. Dried figs, when chopped, can be substituted for raisins in most recipes.

Storage:
Keep fresh ripe figs in plastic in the refrigerator and use them quickly, within 1 or 2 days, because they last only about 1 week after picking. Freeze figs raw or cooked as above for up to 12 months. Dried figs can last for 1 or 2 months if properly covered and refrigerated.

Nutrition:
Figs contain very small amounts of many nu-

trients, including vitamin A, a little bit of calcium and a tiny bit of iron.

FISH AND SHELLFISH

Fish deserves to be part of a young child's diet, but parents often think it is not appropriate because they themselves don't like it or are afraid it may have bones or think it's too hard to cook. The microwave takes all the fuss out of cooking good fish, and for parents who haven't loved fish in the past, trying it on their baby might change their minds, too. Adding fish to your child's diet may have a healthy effect on his adult eating habits, so why not try it now?

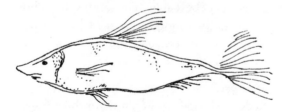

Remember, when preparing fish:
- Fish cooks uniformly, species to species. The thickness and cut are what will affect the cooking times and methods.
- Always watch for bones in those cuts that have them.
- Cook fresh fish within 24 hours of purchase.

- Fish can be the cause of a food allergy. Watch for reactions when it is served for the first time after age 8 or 9 months.
- Cooked fish makes a good finger food.

FILLETS

These are strips of fresh fish cut lengthwise from the bone. Most, if not all, of the bones are removed in the filleting process. You can never be sure that any cut of fish is entirely free of bones, though, so always double-check.

To Cook:
Sprinkle a 4-ounce fillet with water and cook, covered, for 1½ minutes at 100 percent. Let rest, covered, for 2 to 3 minutes before serving.

STEAKS

These are fish portions cut vertically across the fish. Salmon, swordfish, tuna, shark and halibut are all fish species that are frequently cut and sold as steaks. A whole steak will usually weigh in at 8 ounces or more, a portion too large for most children under 2. Cut the steak in half and freeze it if you must, though it's better fresh, or cook it all and have some yourself.

To Cook:

Sprinkle a 3- to 4-ounce steak with water and cook, covered, for 3 minutes at 100 percent. Let rest, covered, for 2 to 3 minutes before serving.

SHELLFISH

I don't feed my girls any shellfish that still has the intestinal tract in it. That means no clams, mussels or oysters, which are all favorites in New England, our part of the country. Lobster and crab can be fed to young children after 10 months, but both are so expensive, and are best prepared boiled or steamed on your stove top, not in the microwave.

SCALLOPS

Scallops are an excellent food for babies. They are rich in protein and have no bones to worry about. Use scallops within 1 day of purchase or keep frozen for up to 3 months.

To Cook:

Arrange 4 ounces of scallops in a circle and cook, covered, at 100 percent for 2 minutes. Let them rest, covered, for 2 to 3 minutes before serving. Serve with a little lemon juice or grated cheese.

SHRIMP

When preparing fresh shrimp for baby, remove the head, shell and both the sand and intestinal tracts. One runs down the back, and the other on the underside by the flippers.

To Cook:

Cook 3 to 4 medium-sized shrimp 3 minutes, covered, at 100 percent. Shrimp, when cooked, turn a pretty pink color because of all the iodine they contain. Let the shrimp rest, covered, for 2 to 3 minutes before serving.

Nutrition:

Fish and shellfish are a very good source of protein, and they can also supply zinc as well as iodine. Eating fish just once a week is credited with reducing heart attacks, and research suggests that the oils in fish have a protective effect.

Comments:

The news about fish is not all positive. Some fishes have been found to be contaminated with chlorinated hydrocarbons and mercury. These chemicals may increase the risk of cancer. Chlorinated hydrocarbons are likely to accumulate in fatty fish. To be safe, avoid serving carp, catfish, lake trout, whitefish, bluefish and striped bass, which are all naturally rich in fat. Mercury may be present in swordfish, halibut, bass, burbot, perch, pike and sheepshead. The consumer group Center for Science in the Public Interest suggests the following fish species as best bets: freshwater—yellow perch, freshwater bass, white perch, brook trout, rainbow trout, lake whitefish, lake trout; saltwater—pink salmon, chum salmon, sockeye salmon, sardines, herring, cod, haddock, pollock, yellowfin tuna, flounder, ocean perch, Pacific halibut, albacore tuna.

GREENS (ESCAROLE, KALE, COLLARDS, BEETS, TURNIPS, DANDELIONS, FIDDLEHEADS)

Buy young tender greens with deep color. If you pick dandelions or fiddleheads in the wild, make sure they are in an area that has not been treated with fertilizers or pesticides.

To Prepare:
Rinse greens very well by actually submerging them in water, as they can collect a lot of dirt.

To Cook:
Cook ½ pound with 2 tablespoons water, covered, at 100 percent for 5 minutes.

Infants:
Chop, then purée with cooking water.

Toddlers:
Chop, then serve with fresh lemon juice.

Storage:
Use greens within 2 days and keep very cold while storing.

Nutrition:
All greens are rich in fiber. In general, the darker the color, the richer the nutrient content.

Comments:
Raw greens are too hard for children under age 2 to chew; save them for later.

GRITS

Grits are probably most popular in the South. They are legendary everywhere else, even among those who have never tasted them. They are made from soaked corn that is dried, then ground. If you are introducing older children to grits, tell them that the cornflakes they enjoy are made by toasting and rolling grits.

To Cook:
Mix 3 tablespoons quick-cooking grits with

¾ cup water, and cook at 100 percent for 2 minutes. Stir, then let rest for 2 minutes. Serve as a rice, potato or noodle substitute, or use as a breakfast cereal, but cook with half milk and half water.

Infants:

Serve with enough liquid so that they are smooth for easy swallowing. Serve after age 8 months.

Toddlers:

Serve as is, or with a dab of butter or margarine.

Storage:

Store in a cool, dry place and use within 1 month for optimal freshness.

Nutrition:

Grits provide some B vitamins.

HONEY

Winnie the Pooh loved honey, but as parents are often surprised to learn, honey is not a good food for all babies. It should not be served to children under 1 year of age either as a sweetener or in baked food. Honey may contain botulism spores that could multiply while in a young infant's intestine. When spores grow, they produce a potent toxin that can cause life-threatening illness. Adults and older children can render these spores harmless if they are ingested.

Nutritionally, honey is not a superior sweetener (see the section on Sugar for a comparison to other sweeteners). If you are a grown-up honey lover and the honey crystallizes, put it in a loosely covered dish, cook it for 30 to 60 seconds at 100 percent and it will liquefy again.

KIWI FRUIT

Kiwi fruit is a pretty fruit that can be served raw when it's ripe. Just peel and cut it into small pieces for a finger food or mash it with a fork. Kiwi fruit has tiny black seeds that are so small they should not be a problem for a 10-month-old to handle easily. Younger children will probably not like the feel of the seeds in their mouth. Kiwi can also be cooked, but don't be surprised that cooking dulls the beautiful emerald color.

To Poach:

Peel and quarter, then add 1 tablespoon juice or water. Cover, then cook at 100 percent for 2 minutes. Mash with a fork or chop.

Infants:

Little ones will probably not like the texture

of the tiny seeds, so try it when they're older.

Toddlers:

Serve fresh, chopped, or cooked and mashed.

Storage:

Like any fruit, kiwis are perishable. Ripen at room temperature, then refrigerate and eat within 2 to 3 days.

Nutrition:

A good source of vitamin C and potassium.

LAMB

When Emily and Sarah were babies, lamb was a favorite food for both. Most babies love it, and we adults should try eating more of this flavorful meat. When cooking lamb for a baby, cook only 1 or 2 ounces at a time. Freeze 2-ounce portions of sliced lamb or buy a pound of ground lamb and freeze it in 8 little balls. This way you'll always have a supply available and won't have to defrost a big piece.

LAMB PATTIES

To Cook:

Shape 2 ounces ground lamb into a thin patty. Cook at 100 percent, covered with a paper towel, for 2 minutes. Cover and let rest 2 to 3 minutes.

LAMB SHANK

To Cook:

To cook a 10-ounce lamb shank, add 2 tablespoons water, cover, and cook at 100 percent for 7 minutes, then let it rest for 5 minutes.

LAMB FOR STEWING

To Prepare:

Cut 2 ounces of lamb from a shank or steak into bite-size pieces. Cover with ¼ cup water, broth or tomato juice (use the tomato juice only if children are older than 10 months).

To Cook:

Cook, uncovered, for 2 minutes at 100 percent. Let rest 3 to 5 minutes. Serve as is, or chop further.

Infants:

Drain cooked lamb, if necessary, then purée with enough reserved liquid to make a smooth purée. Children under 9 months will probably need to have this strained.

Toddlers:
Chop or grind to meet your child's chewing ability. Break lamb patties into bite-size pieces.

Storage:
Uncooked lamb will last 1 to 2 days in the refrigerator and 3 to 4 months frozen.

Nutrition:
An excellent protein and iron source.

LIVER, CHICKEN

We all seem to have memories of being forced to eat liver, but chicken livers, in my opinion, are the tastiest of all meat livers, and your child may really enjoy them. Besides, she is too young to have heard any of the rumors about them! Each time you buy a whole chicken, save the chicken liver and freeze it. Each weighs about 1 ounce, just enough for a small serving. Babies can eat beef and calf's liver, but I prefer chicken because of its taste and easy-to-use portion size.

To Prepare:
Clean and discard any connective tissue or membrane, then slice in half. Prick pieces once or twice with a sharp knife.

To Cook:
Add 1 tablespoon water, cover and cook 2 minutes at 100 percent. Let rest 2 to 3 minutes. Or melt 1 teaspoon butter or margarine for 30 seconds at 100 percent, add sliced livers and coat with the butter. Cook 4 livers 2 to 3 minutes at 100 percent, then cover and let rest for 2 to 3 minutes.

Infants:
Purée poached livers with extra water if needed.

Toddlers:
Mash or chop either poached or sautéed livers.

Storage:
Don't keep livers in the refrigerator too long. When fresh they will last only 1 to 2 days, but they last 2 to 4 months when frozen.

Nutrition:
One of the best sources of iron, and also rich in protein, vitamins and many micronu-

trients. Liver of all types has fallen out of favor because of its high cholesterol value. Despite the cholesterol problem, the American Heart Association gives adults on low-cholesterol diets the okay to eat liver once a month because it is so rich in nutrients.

MAYONNAISE

My oldest daughter loves mayonnaise. At restaurants, if I let her, she would be happy to dip crackers into mayonnaise and just lick it off, without even tasting the cracker.

There is nothing wrong with a toddler having some mayonnaise, but there is no need for mayonnaise in an infant's diet: It's tasty, but not very nutritious. Mayonnaise is made from oil, egg yolk and vinegar, so most of its calories come from fat.

Storage:
Opened jars of mayonnaise must be kept refrigerated. They can last up to 1 year once opened, but should be used within 6 months of the "sell by" date on the label.

Never, ever, allow foods made with mayonnaise to be left at room temperature; because mayonnaise is made with egg, it can spoil and cause illness. This means that when your children are older, don't take deviled eggs and tuna mixed with mayon-

naise on picnics. It's best to leave these traditional picnic foods behind and opt for something safer.

MILK

Milk is an extremely important food for babies. Breast milk is the best first choice, followed by formula. But at some point after your baby is at least 6 months old, you'll substitute other milks for breast milk and formula. Here is a guide that will explain the differences:

RAW MILK

Milk that is not pasteurized. Good dairies regularly inspect their cattle for good health, but even milk from healthy cows can become contaminated if served raw. "Certified Raw Milk" is not a safety guarantee. It means only that the dairy and the workers have met standards. Because of the risk of contamination, raw milk is not advised for infants or young children. It is not as easily digested as other milks because it is not heat treated.

PASTEURIZED MILK

Milk that is heated to kill bacteria and to improve digestibility. It is the milk you'll find in your supermarket. No cow's milk should be served under age 6 months, but if, for some reason, you must, boil pasteurized milk to kill any bacteria that might have grown while sitting in your refrigerator. Be aware that overboiling of milk concentrates it and could potentially upset your child's stomach and cause diarrhea.

HOMOGENIZED MILK

Whole milk that has had the fat broken into minuscule pieces. It has the same fat content throughout, and the fat is evenly distributed, therefore the cream does not rise to the top. Pasteurized, homogenized milk is what most of us buy in the dairy case. Milk that is not homogenized can be easily identified because it has a yummy, rich layer of cream on the surface. Both homogenized and nonhomogenized milk are okay for babies over 6 months old as long as they are pasteurized.

EVAPORATED MILK

Canned milk that has half the water removed. It must be mixed with an equal portion of water before serving. Keep canned milk around for those days you run out of regular milk for drinking or cooking. It can last for months if unopened. Buy milk that has vitamin D added. This is not recommended to be served until age 6 months.

FORMULA

Usually made from cow's milk, it is available in powdered or liquid form. It is designed to mimic breast milk nutritionally and provides about 20 calories per ounce—the same number of calories as breast milk and cow's milk.

CONDENSED MILK

Evaporated milk with a lot of sugar added to it. It is great for making pudding but has no place as an infant's beverage. It is too high in sugar and low in fat and protein to be healthy for babies.

DRIED SKIM MILK

Cow's milk that has had all the liquid removed. It lasts a long time on the shelf without going rancid because it contains very little fat. It is not appropriate for infants or young children. It is inadequate in fat and calories and too high in minerals and proteins, which could damage tiny kidneys. Only babies under a doctor's care because of a fat intolerance may be advised to drink this milk.

ACID AND FERMENTED MILKS

Milk products that have had natural acids added or are fermented by the addition of a lactic-acid-producing organism. These milks are seldom recommended for infants.

GOAT'S MILK

This milk is usually tried if a child has an intolerance to cow's milk, but a child with a cow's milk allergy may still be allergic to goat's milk. In other countries, however, its use is commonplace. It is very digestible, but naturally low in vitamin D, iron and folic acid. The American Academy of Pediatrics recommends that infants not be fed a steady diet of this milk because of its nutritional inadequacies. Boil goat's milk before feeding it to infants.

IMITATION MILKS

The white nondairy liquids and powders you add to your coffee. They may look like they come from a cow, but they don't. They come from a chemist and have none of the nutritional benefits that milk does. Youngsters fed these cream substitutes in place of milk run a high risk of becoming malnourished.

SPECIALTY MILKS AND FORMULAS

Commercial formulas and milk products with specific nutritional modifications. Such products may have modified amounts of protein, carbohydrates, even fat and sodium. In most cases the substitutes are needed only for someone who has medical problems. They are expensive and should be used under the guidance of a physician or a registered dietitian.

MILLET

Millet is a tiny yellow grain that is showing up more and more in markets, restaurants and even on the family table. It has a very mild flavor and tastes best if cooked in broth or mixed with other foods. My girls like millet, but it isn't something we cook as frequently as we might some other surefire favorites, such as rice. Try the recipe below. Your children may find it to be a real winner, and it's easy to cook, too.

To Prepare:
Mix ½ cup millet with 1½ cups liquid (water, juice or broth) in a 4-cup bowl.

To Cook:
Cook, uncovered, for 5 minutes at 100 percent. Stir, cover and cook on the lowest

setting for 10 minutes. If it still has an un-cooked taste, cook again for 2 minutes (add ½ cup more liquid if it looks dry) and let rest 5 minutes. It should be soft, tender and mushy.

Infants:
Serve with applesauce or yogurt after age 8 months. It is a small grain and does not need puréeing, but it should be mushy, not dry.

Toddlers:
Serve in place of rice or potatoes.

Storage:
Keep stored in a plastic bag in the refrigerator. Use within 1 month. Millet that is old seems to take longer to cook. To increase your chances of purchasing fresh millet, try to buy it in a store that has a good turnover rate.

Nutrition:
Millet will not knock anyone over with its nutritional content. However, it is a primary staple in Africa and India.

MOLASSES

Molasses is made from the juice of sugar-cane, which is then purified and boiled. There are three commercial varieties: light, dark and blackstrap. Light and dark molasses have a taste that I like and even consider for use as a maple-syrup replacement on pancakes. In my opinion, blackstrap molasses is too awful-tasting to serve to anyone, particularly babies. Though it is credited traditionally with superior nutritional merits, most of these claims are exaggerated.

Storage:
Molasses can be kept for a year before it's opened. Once opened, keep it in the refrigerator and use within 6 to 12 months.

Nutrition:
See Sugar for a nutritional comparison of molasses to other sweeteners, and try Indian Pudding (see page 191) for a yummy treat.

MUSHROOMS

Every time I pull out mushrooms for cooking, my 2-year-old daughter asks for a taste. She finds something about mushrooms appealing, but the result is always the same: She chews a little, then spits it out. But when they're cooked in butter or served in a stew, she always scrapes her plate.

To Prepare:
Remove any dirt by brushing with a paper towel. Slice into bite-size pieces.

To Cook:

For 1 cup of sliced mushrooms, melt 1 teaspoon butter by cooking at 100 percent for 30 seconds. Mix in mushrooms. Cook, covered, 3 minutes.

Infants:

Nutritionally, mushrooms just don't warrant a place in your baby's diet. Hold off until 12 months.

Toddlers:

Serve the above recipe chopped to meet baby's chewing ability.

Storage:

Keep refrigerated and use within 2 or 3 days, before they darken and their surfaces get slimy.

Nutrition:

Mushrooms contain small amounts of vitamins and minerals.

NUTS

For children under 2 years of age, I don't like to see nuts as part of their diet. They are hard and difficult to chew, particularly in mouths that still don't have a full set of teeth. Even at age 3, when your child has most of his first teeth, I still worry about choking. Nuts are a very good protein source, but I think it's best to serve them ground up, as in peanut butter, not in whole form (see Peanut Butter).

OAT BRAN

As soon as the cereal corporations learned that we liked the idea of eating a cereal that could lower cholesterol, they really started to promote this product. Now oat bran is on everything, even added to potato chips! I'm surprised but pleased to find that there is not an oat-bran cereal marketed for infants. Research studies have demonstrated that oat bran in the diet can lower blood-cholesterol levels in adults. Recently it has been suggested, however, that the reason it lowers cholesterol is because it replaces high-fat, high-cholesterol breakfast items such as eggs and bacon in the diet and not because it has any unique abilities. The debate about the merits of oat bran is sure to continue. What I do know for sure is that eating oat bran alone does not ensure good health. It must be part of a total health program to do the job it is credited with. Infants and toddlers can have oat-bran cereal, but I don't advise a steady diet of it. A cereal such as oat bran that is rich in fiber might interfere with the absorption of important nutrients if large servings were consumed every day. If you want to serve oat bran, I would recommend that you rotate serving it with other hot cereals so that baby has it only a few times a week.

To Prepare:
Mix ¾ cup water with ⅓ cup oat bran.

To Cook:
Cook, uncovered, at 100 percent for 3 minutes. Stir after 1 minute. Cover and let rest 1 minute.

Infants:
Serve diluted with infant juice or formula.

Toddlers:
Serve like oatmeal.

Storage:
Keep in a cool, dry place. It will last a long time if well covered or refrigerated.

Nutrition:
Rich in water-soluble fiber.

OATMEAL

This is a favorite with my kids, and with the microwave, it's a snap. I prefer the flavor of old-fashioned oatmeal to instant, and since cooking in the microwave is so speedy, I really don't even see the need for instant. If you're using the instant varieties, please hold off on the flavored types. These are loaded with sugar, and once started you'll have a tough time ever getting your little one to eat the unsweetened kind.

OLD-FASHIONED OATMEAL

To Prepare:
Mix ¾ cup water with ⅓ cup old-fashioned oatmeal.

To Cook:
Cook at 100 percent, uncovered, for 3 minutes, stir and then let stand 1 minute covered.

INSTANT OATMEAL

To Prepare:
Mix packet with ⅔ cup water, stir.

To Cook:
Cook, uncovered, at 100 percent for 1½ to 2 minutes.

Infants:
Purée with apple juice or formula.

Toddlers:
Serve with added milk, fruit or sweetener, if desired.

Storage:
Old-fashioned oatmeal should be used within a month to ensure maximum freshness. Keep it in the refrigerator.

Nutrition:
Oatmeal contains some protein, a small amount of iron (unless it's iron-fortified) and some of the B vitamins.

ONIONS

Onions are another one of those vegetables that my girls like the look of, but when they taste them they make faces. In recipes like stews, soups and casseroles, onions do a wonderful job of adding flavor. I can see no reason why a child as young as 8 months couldn't have onions, if chopped small, in a cooked dinner. I don't serve cooked onions as a vegetable to my girls, but I don't know why you shouldn't. In case your child likes onions served as a vegetable, I offer the following cooking instructions.

To Prepare:
Peel and chop 1 small onion into bite-size pieces.

To Cook:
Melt 1 teaspoon butter by cooking at 100 percent for 1 minute. Toss in onions and distribute butter well. Cook, covered, for 3 minutes.

Infants:
Not recommended.

Toddlers:
Serve cooked and chopped.

Storage:
Store in baskets or bags so that air can circulate. They can last 2 to 4 weeks.

Nutrition:
Onions contain small amounts of several nutrients but are not powerhouse suppliers of any.

ORANGES

Oranges are pretty, delicious and nutritious. Unfortunately, young children seem to have trouble eating orange sections. If you have patience, free the fruit from the peel and cut out the membranes that keep them together. Then serve chunks of orange to your child. Canned mandarin oranges have very tender membranes and are easily chewed or gummed by little ones. There is no need to cook oranges, so just serve them raw.

Infants:
Hold off on orange juice or orange pieces until at least 8 months because of the chance of a food reaction.

Toddlers:
Orange juice is one of the best breakfast drinks, and fresh orange wedges and slices are a real treat for all children over 8 months. Just make sure you serve them cut up into a form that matches your child's chewing ability.

Nutrition:
Oranges are a great source of vitamin C. One orange contains 60 to 100 milligrams, and a glass of juice contains 60 to 80 milligrams. Studies show that even after 20 days, a 6-ounce glass of refrigerated orange juice, made from concentrate, still contains 50 milligrams of vitamin C. A young child needs 35 to 40 milligrams daily.

PAPAYA

A ripe, soft papaya makes an ideal instant baby food. It is very sweet and easy to eat, and it can be served raw when ripe. If you want to rush the ripening along, the microwave can help.

To Ripen:
Prick skin. Cook whole at 100 percent for 1 minute, then let rest until cool.

Infants:
Slice in half, remove and discard the black seeds. Scoop out the fruit and mash or purée with added fruit juice.

Toddlers:
Slice as above but serve mashed or cut into chunks.

Storage:
A papaya can last for 1 to 2 weeks, depending on how ripe and soft it was when you brought it home. Refrigerate when ripe.

Nutrition:
Papaya is a very good source of vitamins A and C.

PARSNIPS

This vegetable looks like a white carrot and has a sweet, appealing taste. Children like it in stews and casseroles or served as a vegetable just as you would serve a carrot. Mashed with cooked carrots and some butter, it is known in England as Bash.

If you buy very large parsnips, they may have woody, tough centers that must be cut out, so look for the smaller ones.

To Prepare:
Peel and chop into small pieces.

To Cook:
Cook 1 cup chopped parsnips with ½ cup water at 100 percent, covered, for 4 minutes. Let rest 5 minutes. The vegetables must be soft, so that they can be easily mashed with a fork.

Infants:
Purée with water, juice or milk if your child is old enough.

Toddlers:
Serve mashed or puréed.

Storage:
Keep parsnips refrigerated in plastic for 7 to 10 days. Cooked parsnips can be kept for 2 to 3 days, or freeze up to 10 months.

Nutrition:
Parsnips contain some vitamin A and lots of good fiber.

PEANUT BUTTER

Peanut butter is universally identified as a kids' food. You can try it as early as age 8 months. Peanuts are a common food allergen, so keep a watchful eye the first time you offer it.

Peanut butter is made by puréeing peanuts, but not all peanut butters are created equal. Most commercial varieties have a good deal of added sugar, salt and fats to keep them stabilized, and chances are the peanut butter you introduce your child to now will be the one he will always identify as his own. I recommend the ones without added salt or sugar. These are the brands that have no stabilizers, and so the oil rises to the top. By stirring the peanut butter or flipping the jar over from time to time, you can keep the oil fairly well distributed. Kept cold in the refrigerator, the oil won't separate out, either.

Infants:
Hold off until at least 8 months and then serve in very small amounts. Slices of bread spread with peanut butter can become one large glob in the mouth, so please be careful. I would recommend tearing up the bread or sandwich into bite-size pieces, and then keeping a careful eye out that your little one doesn't stuff too much in at once.

Toddlers:
A peanut butter sandwich, of course, is the hands-down preferred method. Include small amounts of jelly if you like, or, better

yet, replace jelly with sliced banana or chopped canned fruit.

Storage:
Unopened peanut butter can last for a year. Once opened, refrigerate, particularly in very hot weather, and use within 3 or 4 months.

Nutrition:
Peanuts are a good protein source. They are also rich in calories—1 tablespoon of peanut butter supplies 100 calories.

Comments:
If your pocketbook can take it, there are other nut butters, too. Cashew and almond butters are delicious but expensive.

A September 1990 article in *Consumer Reports* reported that fresh ground peanut butters were more likely to contain harmful aflatoxin than supermarket peanut butters. Aflatoxin is a naturally occurring poison that increases cancer risk. Of the tested brands, Jif, Skippy, Peter Pan, and Smucker's had the lowest levels of aflatoxin.

PEARS

Pears are one of my family's favorite fruits. A delicious ripe pear served at room temperature is fabulous. It can also be cooked and served with yogurt or, for a special treat, with ice cream.

To Prepare:
Slice in half, cut out seeds and core (if serving to an infant, peel), lay both sides cut side down, add ½ cup water, cover.

To Cook:
Cook 3 minutes at 100 percent, covered.

Infants:
Purée peeled, cooked fruit with juice or water.

Toddlers:
Serve chopped or mashed.

Storage:
Ripe fruit lasts 3 to 5 days. Allow fruit to ripen at room temperature.

Nutrition:
A good source of fiber, and they contain vitamins A and C as well as potassium.

PEAS

Peas are a favorite vegetable for most kids. They are round, bright and fun to play with. Slightly flattened, they make a good finger food for beginning eaters. Unfortunately, when your child is around the 18- to 24-

month mark, he may discover that they are wonderful to throw, too!

FRESH PEAS

To Prepare:
Remove from pod. (Try to let your 18-month-old help.)

To Cook:
Cook 1 cup with 1 tablespoon water at 100 percent, covered, for 3 minutes. The peas should be soft.

FROZEN PEAS

To Cook:
If right from the freezer, cook ½ cup, covered and sprinkled with water, about 2 to 3 minutes. If thawed, warm only by heating at 100 percent for 30 seconds.

Infants:
Purée with extra water and press through a strainer or food mill.

Toddlers:
Serve in a bowl with a spoon, or mash with a fork if they are too frustrating for your little one to keep on a spoon.

Storage:
Fresh peas last 3 to 4 days in the refrigerator or 10 to 12 months if frozen.

Nutrition:
Peas are a good source of vitamin A and fiber.

PEPPERS

Fresh, crisp bell peppers make lovely snacks for children who have enough teeth to chew. Cooked and puréed, they make refreshing sauces for serving over noodles or rice. (See recipe for Sarah's Rice with Red or Green Pepper Sauce and Cheese, page 151.)

To Prepare:
Use any color pepper, but red is the sweetest. Remove core and seeds, cut into strips. Put in a microwave-safe dish with 1 tablespoon water.

To Cook:
Cook 1 chopped pepper, covered, for about 4 minutes. It should become limp.

Infants:

Purée the whole cooked pepper with water and push through a strainer to remove any pieces of skin.

Toddlers:

Cut cooked peppers into bite-size pieces and serve as a vegetable. Raw pepper can also be served in bite-size pieces.

Storage:

Fresh peppers can last 3 or 4 days. Keep refrigerated.

Nutrition:

A very good source of vitamin C.

Comments:

Bell peppers have no capsaicin, the hot substance found in chili peppers that gives them their distinctive taste. Though many cultures include chili peppers as part of a young

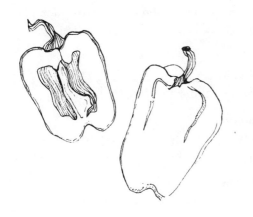

child's diet, I am reluctant to recommend it because they can "burn" an uninitiated eater. (The oils that create "heat" in the mouth can also irritate eyes if they make contact, so although you don't serve them to your baby, be cautious anyway whenever chili peppers are around.)

Black and white pepper as a seasoning is not on my recommended list for young children, either. This type of pepper can be a stomach irritant and, though flavorful, ground pepper has no place on your child's menu before age 2.

PINEAPPLE

A ripe room-temperature piece of pineapple is a wonderful dessert for children with teeth. I never fed fresh pineapple to my children until about 18 months because it's so fibrous. Canned pineapple (look for the kind with no sugar added) is more tender, probably because it is heated during the canning process.

Most pineapple is served without cooking, but if you want to warm it up to perhaps soften it, try the following method.

To Prepare:

Slice off top of pineapple, then cut away skin by cutting lengthwise with a knife.

Quarter, then cut out the hard center core and cut the fruit into cubes.

To Cook:
Cook 1 cup pineapple cubes, covered, for 3 minutes at 100 percent.

Infants:
Not recommended for the very young, but try puréed or mashed at age 10 months.

Toddlers:
Serve raw in cubes or sliced, or cooked and mashed. Serve with plain yogurt or a little ice cream while still warm.

Storage:
Fresh pineapple will keep 4 to 5 days. It should have a slight sweet pineapple smell when ripe.

Nutrition:
An excellent source of vitamin C and fiber.

PLUMS

Plums come in many colors and sizes. Always remove the pit when serving to a child under age 5 or 6. The pits are small, slippery and could easily be swallowed. Prunes are dried plums, and both are Mother Nature's natural laxatives. They can be good if your child is a little constipated. If, on the other hand, you're going to be traveling and diaper changing will be difficult, do not bring plums as a snack!

Plums are usually eaten raw, but they are delicious and easily prepared in the microwave. (See recipe for Plums with Yogurt, page 126.) Puréeing is easier when cooked.

To Prepare:
Slice in half, remove pit, place cut side down, add 1 tablespoon water, cover.

To Cook:
Cook 2½ minutes at 100 percent. To remove skins, carefully take the hot plums from the oven and remove peel with a fork.

Infants:
Remove skin, then purée with juice plums were cooked in and additional water if needed.

Toddlers:
Serve chopped with or without skins.

Storage:
Plums last 3 to 5 days refrigerated. Cooked and frozen, they can last 10 to 12 months.

Nutrition:
Very rich in potassium and vitamin A.

POLENTA (SEE CORNMEAL)

PORK

Today's pork is leaner than its ancestors, but the potential for trichinosis is still present. Whenever you're cooking pork, cook it until it's very hot, with an internal temperature of 170 degrees. You can test the temperature with a small meat thermometer. When cooking pork for babies in the microwave, cut it into small pieces so it gets heated all the way through.

To Prepare:
Trim fat from a pork chop or a pork steak. Cut a 2-ounce piece into ¼-inch bite-size cubes.

To Cook:
Cover and cook with ¼ cup water, tomato juice or beef broth for 2 minutes at 100 percent. It must be steaming hot. Stir and let rest 5 minutes.

Infants:
Purée with added water and strain.

Toddlers:
Serve as is with vegetable and a starch.

Storage:
Keeps for 1 to 2 days in the refrigerator and 2 months in the freezer.

Nutrition:
A good protein and iron source.

Comments:
Cured pork is what most of us think of when we talk about ham. The curing process adds a significant amount of sodium as well as unwanted preservatives. Because of the high sodium level, I don't recommend feeding babies ham at all. If you want to give some to your toddler, serve it chopped and only occasionally because of the sodium.

POTATOES

Potatoes are wonderful for children because they cook quickly, they come individually wrapped in their own skin, and toddlers love to eat them plain.

To Prepare:
Wash and prick skins.

To Cook:
Cook 1 potato for 5 minutes at 100 percent. It should feel hot and soft when cooked.

Infants:
In order to make potatoes smooth and creamy, mix with formula or use milk if your baby is at least 6 months old. Sometimes young children don't like the grainy texture

of potatoes, so if this is true in your house, just try them again when a little older.

Toddlers:
Cooked potatoes can be cut into chunks and eaten as a finger food, or mash with a fork and add milk and a little butter.

Storage:
Potatoes can last 2 to 8 weeks if they are kept in a cool, dark spot.

Nutrition:
A good source of vitamin C, fiber and potassium.

Comments:
Carefully trim off any of the eyes, sprouts, bruises or green spots that might appear on the potato skins. These areas can be a concentrated source of naturally occurring glycoalkaloids, which, if consumed in very large amounts, can cause illness such as headache, nausea or diarrhea.

RAISINS

Raisins are dried grapes, and as any parent knows, they are very popular with kids. They need no cooking, but you can "plump" them up if you like.

To Cook:
Mix ½ cup raisins with 1 tablespoon water, cover and cook for 1 minute at 100 percent. Use puréed cooked raisins to fill tart shells or spread on a cookie or cracker.

Infants:
Not recommended for infants in dry form because they are hard to chew. Could be served if cooked, but the raisin "mash" is still tricky for babies because it is so sticky. Better to wait until 12 months.

Toddlers:
Serve uncooked as a snack or in the above recipe as suggested.

Storage:
They keep about 1 month at room temperature, and, tightly covered, up to 6 months in the refrigerator.

Nutrition:
Raisins contain a little calcium and are a very good source of potassium.

RHUBARB

If you have a garden that faithfully produces rhubarb every year, then you will want to feed it to baby (and anyone else who is around) just to get rid of it. Rhubarb is a vegetable that has the same appearance and cooking characteristics as celery, but most cooks treat it as a fruit. It must have sugar added to it to make it palatable. Never let little ones chew on the leaves, as they are rich in oxalic acid, which could make them sick.

To Prepare:
Chop stems into bite-size pieces.

To Cook:
Mix 1 cup finely chopped rhubarb with 1 tablespoon white sugar and cook, covered, 2 minutes at 100 percent. Let sit until cool, then purée or mash. Cook 1 or 2 minutes longer if not tender.

Infants:
Rhubarb cooks into a nice purée, but I think it is too tart for little ones.

Toddlers:
Serve as is, or over ice cream, cottage cheese or even yogurt, or mix with cooked fruits.

Storage:
Refrigerate for 3 to 5 days. Freeze cooked rhubarb for 10 to 12 months.

Nutrition:
Contains some calcium, potassium, and vitamin A. It is very low in calories and has a lot of fiber.

RICE

To cook rice properly, the grains must be allowed to absorb water. The microwave can cook rice nicely. Much of the cooking time is actually spent resting and not in the oven cooking. This recipe uses more liquid than usual. I find that my kids like rice very tender and moist.

WHITE RICE

To Prepare:
Mix ½ cup rice with 1¼ cups water in a 4-cup bowl so that water doesn't boil out.

To Cook:
Cook 5 minutes, uncovered, at 100 percent, then let rest 15 minutes, covered. Stir and

cook 2 to 3 minutes more at 100 percent, uncovered. Let rest 2 to 3 minutes, covered, until tender and most of the liquid is absorbed.

INSTANT RICE

This is a parboiled rice that has sacrificed flavor for fast cooking, but it saves time so I occasionally use it. Both the long-cooking and the instant rice are fortified with the same nutrients.

To Prepare:
Mix ⅔ cup rice with ⅔ cup water.

To Cook:
Cover and cook at 100 percent for 4 minutes in a 4-cup bowl. Fluff before serving.

BROWN RICE

Brown rice has not had its high-fiber outside cover removed—hence the brown color. It is more nutritious than white rice, but it takes much longer to cook. In most cases I would recommend that you cook brown rice on the stove top and put some aside for baby, or even freeze cooked brown rice so that you have it when you need it. Cooking information for the microwave is included in case you want to prepare it this way.

To Prepare:
Mix ½ cup brown rice with 1½ cups water in a 4-cup dish.

To Cook:
Cook 5 minutes, covered, at 100 percent. Stir, then let rest 10 minutes. Cook 5 minutes more, then let rest 15 minutes. Always keep it covered. If the rice still needs additional cooking, cook at 2-minute increments and add more water if it appears dry.

INSTANT BROWN RICE

Just as I was finishing the final editing on this book, I learned that two major companies were marketing an instant brown rice, so I tried it. It cooked in 10 minutes and tasted good. Not as good as the longer cooking kind, but still good. Most important, I gave it to Sarah and Emily and they ate it all!

To Prepare:
Mix ⅔ cup water with ½ cup rice.

To Cook:

Cover and cook at 100 percent for 2 minutes. Stir and cook for 3 minutes at medium power, then let rest for 3 to 4 minutes until tender.

WILD RICE

This is really a grain shaped like rice and not a true rice. It is expensive and time-consuming to cook, but tasty when cooked with a flavorful liquid, so you might want to try it on your toddlers.

To Cook:

Mix ½ cup wild rice with 1½ cups liquid (broth or half-strength juice) in a 4-cup bowl. Cook, uncovered, 5 minutes at 100 percent, stir, let rest 10 minutes, covered, stir, cook 5 minutes, uncovered, and let rest until tender.

Infants:

Purée cooked rice when offering it for the first time, then try it mushed with fruit or yogurt and finally whole. It is doubtful that babies will appreciate wild rice, so don't waste it on them, but they usually love all other varieties.

Toddlers:

Serve as is with a little dab of butter or some cooked fruit or applesauce.

Storage:

All uncooked rice lasts almost indefinitely when stored in a cool, dry spot. If keeping brown rice for more than a month, store in the refrigerator.

Nutrition:

Rice is rich in B vitamins. White rice has iron added to it, while brown rice contains more fiber.

SPINACH

Kids have a funny reaction to spinach. It can be runny and mysterious-looking, and thus unappealing, but, on the other hand, Popeye eats lots of it and that might help you build a case in its favor—at least when your child is a little older. Kids often enjoy it mixed in with soups and egg dishes, but still refuse it served alone.

To Prepare:

Wash and trim stems. You may want to rinse it twice, as the sandy soil it grows in clings quite tenaciously to its leaves.

To Cook:

Sprinkle ¼ pound with water and cook 4 minutes, covered, at 100 percent.

Infants:

Purée and strain.

Toddlers:
Serve chopped. Add a little grated nutmeg for special flavor.

Storage:
Fresh spinach should be washed and stored in plastic and used within 1 to 2 days. Frozen, it can last for 6 months or more.

Nutrition:
It is a very rich vitamin A and fiber source and contains some calcium as well. It also contains oxalic acid, a natural substance that may block calcium absorption. To prevent any problems, don't serve more than once a day.

SQUASH

A wonderful food that can be popped into the oven and needs very little fussing, squash is a real kid-pleaser. (See Zucchini for summer squash.)

To Prepare:
Slice an acorn or butternut squash in half, remove seeds, place cut side down.

To Cook:
Cook, uncovered, at 100 percent. For an acorn half, about 7 minutes. For a butternut half, about 10 minutes. Cooking times de-pend on size. If the squash is still firm when pierced with a fork, cook 2 minutes longer. When the flesh is tender, hold the squash with a heat-proof mitt and scrape out the pulp.

Infants:
Purée with added water.

Toddlers:
Mash with a fork, add butter and milk or orange juice.

Storage:
A squash can last 2 to 6 weeks if stored in a cool, dry spot. Cooked and frozen, it can keep 10 to 12 months.

Nutrition:
Very rich in vitamin A.

STRAWBERRIES

Strawberries are beautiful, tasty and naturally sweet. They are usually eaten fresh, but they can be cooked in the microwave to make a nice fruit sauce for young children.

To Prepare:
Remove the stems and slice enough to equal ½ cup.

To Cook:
Cook, covered, for 1 minute at 100 percent.

Infants:
Serve puréed or mashed, but do not serve until older than 8 months to reduce the risk of an allergic reaction. Serve as a finger food when able to.

Toddlers:
Older kids usually like their berries fresh and sliced into bite-size pieces.

Storage:
Use berries quickly. They spoil fast and will last only 2 to 4 days in the refrigerator.

Nutrition:
An excellent vitamin C source.

SUGAR

Plain white table sugar has few if any redeeming nutritional qualities, but it does help things taste good! The following is a comparison of the most common sweeteners available per 1 tablespoon serving. None of the sweeteners listed is a nutrition powerhouse, so always use them sparingly.

Sugar	45 calories; only very small traces of nutrients
Honey	65 calories; a tiny bit of iron, calcium and sodium
Brown sugar	52 calories; small amounts of sodium, potassium, iron and calcium
Barley malt syrup	59 calories; a very small amount of iron and calcium
Turbinado sugar	48 calories; 1 mg iron
Molasses (light)	50 calories, 16 mg sodium, 300 mg potassium, .9 mg iron, 33 mg calcium
Black strap molasses	43 calories; 2.3 mg iron, 116 mg calcium
Maple syrup	50 calories; a small amount of potassium and calcium, and just a little smidge of iron

SWEET POTATOES

The sweet potato is always my standby. I keep one or two in the refrigerator at all times. When I'm really in a rush I just prick the skin, cook it in minutes, then serve it with a little cottage cheese, perhaps a slice of bread and some chopped tomatoes along with a glass of milk or juice to drink. It is always a winner with my kids.

To Prepare:
Wash and prick skin.

To Cook:
Cook 1 potato 7 minutes, uncovered, or until it feels soft.

Infants:
Purée with apple juice or milk after 6 months.

Toddlers:
Mash with a fork, add some milk and a little butter. Can also be cut into cubes as a snack or finger food.

Storage:
Fresh sweet potatoes may last only 2 to 3 days in the refrigerator, so use quickly.

Nutrition:
An excellent source of fiber and vitamin A.

TAPIOCA

As a kid I always loved this dessert, and every time I make it I think of my own mother and childhood. It is made with egg and milk, so hold off making it for your little eater until at least 8 to 10 months of age.

To Prepare:
See recipe on page 188.

Infants:
No, because of the milk.

Toddlers:
Serve as a dessert.

Storage:
Keep in a cool, dry spot and it will last a long time.

Nutrition:
When prepared with milk and egg it is a rich calcium and protein food.

TOFU

To many parents this is an unfamiliar food. You'll usually find it in the produce section of the supermarket, though it should be stored in the dairy case, where it is colder. It is made from soybeans and looks like a block of white cheese submerged in water. It has a bland, subtle flavor that many kids really like. It can be eaten without additional cooking, but cooking will kill any harmful bacteria that may be present.

To Prepare:
Cut into ¼-inch cubes.

To Cook:
Warm until hot in the microwave or combine with leftover rice and vegetables and reheat.

Infants:

Hold off until 8 months of age (a child could be allergic to the soy protein), then serve mashed as a protein serving.

Toddlers:

Serve cooked as a finger food or mashed.

Storage:

Tofu is a perishable item. Make sure it is fresh. If it is vacuum-packed, use by the expiration date on the package. Tofu is often sold in open bins at health-food stores and Oriental markets. If it is purchased this way, the potential for spoilage is present. Ask the store manager how old the tofu is and how frequently the water is changed (it should be changed daily). Tofu can be frozen for up to 2 months.

Nutrition:

Contains protein, iron, calcium and some B vitamins.

Comments:

I was recently delighted to discover a healthy alternative to hot dogs. Tofu Pups, made from tofu, look and (almost) taste like the hot dog we all know and like. It is, however, much lower in saturated fat and sodium and is a better choice for toddlers than hot dogs are. Always slice lengthwise to reduce the risk of choking. To cook one Tofu Pup, prick with a fork and cook 45 seconds at 100 percent.

TOMATOES

If I want my kids to eat something, all I need to do is add tomato sauce to it and they love it. Fresh tomatoes make a wonderful finger food for early eaters and are a great way to get vitamin C.

Fresh tomatoes can be chopped and served as is. Most children 10 months and older can handle the seeds and the skin, providing the tomato is chopped into bite-size pieces.

Infants:

Hold off on fresh tomatoes and even tomato sauces until at least 8 months.

Toddlers:

Serve fresh tomatoes chopped.

TOMATO SAUCE

To Cook:
Core and slice 4 tomatoes in half. Cook, covered, for 8 minutes at 100 percent. Pass through a food mill or purée. Pour into a bowl and cook again for 2 minutes. Freeze in ½-cup portions for use in recipes.

Infants:
Too young.

Toddlers:
Serve cooked tomato sauce over noodles, sliced bread, even cooked rice.

Storage:
Fresh ripe tomatoes should be stored in the refrigerator and used within 2 to 5 days. Green tomatoes can be held at room temperature. Don't ripen in the sun; they get too hot and turn mushy, not red.

Nutrition:
An exceptional source of vitamin C, potassium and fiber. Read about tomato products in Chapter 3.

TUNA

A can of tuna could probably be found in 90 percent of American households. However, it's not a good food for infants because it is not easy to eat. Once a child starts on finger foods, canned tuna can be a protein source that's easy to serve. Babies and toddlers do not need to have mayonnaise added (try using plain yogurt to replace some or all of the mayonnaise). I recommend that you buy tuna canned in water and that it be rinsed before feeding to baby. Rinsing removes some of the sodium but not any of the protein, which is what you serve it for.

See Fish for cooking fresh tuna.

Infants:
Try as a finger food at about 8 months, but at this young age it's still unpopular in many households.

Toddlers:
Tuna makes great sandwiches, served on bread or crackers.

TURKEY

Turkey is wonderful for babies and children, and especially during the holidays we all have plenty of it around.

To Prepare:
Remove skin. Cook on the bone.

To Cook:
Cook 1 drumstick for 7 minutes, covered, at 100 percent until steaming hot. Cook 1 breast for 8 minutes, covered, at 100 percent

until steaming hot. Let rest for 5 minutes, covered, to allow for complete cooking. Never serve pink turkey. It isn't cooked enough.

Storage:
Serve and store as you would cooked chicken.

Comments:
Many packages of ground turkey contain ground skin along with the meat, which means you're getting more fat and less protein. If you want to avoid buying ground-up skin, look for labels that state "turkey meat."

TURNIPS

Turnips are a flavorful root vegetable that cooks beautifully in the microwave.

To Prepare:
Peel and chop into small, uniform cubes. Add 1 tablespoon water per cup diced turnips.

To Cook:
Cook 1 cup diced turnips, covered, for 5 minutes at 100 percent. Let rest 3 minutes. If the turnip is not tender when pierced with a knife, cook for another 2 minutes. Make sure there is still water available for cooking.

Infants:
Purée with added juice, water or milk (when old enough). The flavor is strong and may not be a winner the first time, but try again when your baby is older.

Toddlers:
Serve mashed with a fork. Add in cooked, mashed potato or even cooked fruit.

Storage:
Store fresh turnips refrigerated in plastic for 1 week.

Nutrition:
A good vitamin A and fiber source.

YAMS

I would be hard pressed to distinguish a sweet potato from a yam. Botanically they're different, but their appearance, flavor and cooking methods are nearly identical and so are the nutrients they contain. See Sweet Potatoes for cooking directions.

YOGURT

Yogurt has all the nutrition of a glass of milk, and is credited with many health benefits because it contains friendly bacteria.

These bacteria turn milk from a liquid to a thick and creamy consistency that is easy for babies to eat. Whether it can help us live a hundred years—as some proponents claim—could be debated, but what I do know is that my kids love the creamy, cool taste of plain yogurt. Most parents assume their kids won't like plain yogurt, but offer it that way before serving the sweetened brands. Keep in mind that many flavored, sugared yogurts get half their calories from the added sugar flavorings.

To make a cream cheese look-alike, try this: Drain yogurt overnight in a colander lined with cheesecloth. The result is a yogurt cheese that spreads like cream cheese, but unlike cream cheese it is loaded with calcium and protein.

Infants:
Serve as early as 6 months, plain or mixed with applesauce.

Toddlers:
Serve in place of milk, or use it to mix with cooked fruits or to make noodle or rice dishes moister.

Storage:
Use by the expiration date on the container.

Nutrition:
Like milk, it is rich in calcium, protein and riboflavin.

Comments:
When cooked it usually separates and becomes a bit watery. If your child refuses milk, try yogurt flavored with fruit, such as Plums with Yogurt (see page 126).

ZUCCHINI

As any gardener knows, zucchini grows like a weed, so babies and grown-ups get a lot of it in summer and fall. Zucchini and yellow summer squash share the same cooking times and methods. If blindfolded, I don't believe I could identify or taste the difference between them. The older and bigger a squash gets, the larger and tougher its seeds get, too. Infants should not be fed the seeds, but toddlers can be served zucchini with seeds if they are the tiny ones that come from the young, smaller squash.

To Prepare:
Trim ends, scrub skin. Chop, place in a microwave-safe dish, sprinkle with water and cover.

To Cook:
Cook 1 cup chopped zucchini at 100 percent for 3 minutes.

Infants:
For very young first-time eaters, remove all

seeds, no matter how small. Purée squash, including skin, with water or juice.

Toddlers:
Chop or mash with added butter.

Storage:
Fresh summer squash can last up to a week if kept cold and covered. Cook and freeze for up to 6 months.

Nutrition:
When fresh-picked it is a good vitamin C source, but the vitamin C diminishes with each day of storage.

MARVELOUS

PART 3

MIXTURES

 In the chapters that follow you will find more than fifty healthy recipes to introduce your baby to. I've included variations for most recipes, so these fifty can become the foundation of all the cooking you do for your baby and child. This will also help you if you simply don't have the right ingredients in the house!

As you know, when you first start to feed your little one you will serve only single-ingredient items. Use "My Top One Hundred" to find out how to cook almost everything, from apples to zucchini. But after six months you can start to use the recipes in this section. I've tried to take some of the hassle out of serving "balanced" meals by developing recipes that are complete meals in one dish. And when all the food groups aren't in a main-dish meal, I've included simple suggestions for rounding out the nutrition. You'll notice I've overlapped the ages that the recipes are appropriate for. For instance, the "Something Simple" recipes for age six to ten months overlap with the "Wet and Lumpy" chapter for age eight to twelve months. The reason is that not all children develop at the same rate. And many children will continue to enjoy their favorite "baby" foods when they're much older.

7

SOMETHING SIMPLE

FOR SIX- TO TEN-MONTH-OLDS

 When baby gets a little older (as early as six months), try a recipe from this section. Do not feed your baby two new foods at once. If you do and she has an allergic reaction, you won't be able to identify which food caused the trouble. These recipes are not for balanced meals and they don't really need to be. Your baby should still be getting most of her nutrition from her milk feeding. The recipes will teach your baby to begin enjoying food, though, and they'll introduce you to the pleasure of cooking for your little one.

PLUMS WITH YOGURT

Makes about
½-cup portion
If you are
freezing this, do
so before
adding yogurt.

This is a sweet and yummy treat. To prevent an allergic reaction to the yogurt, serve it after your baby has had his six-month birthday. Keep in mind that plums when dried are prunes, and both can act as a natural laxative!

> *2 plums, about 2 inches in diameter, any color or variety*
> *½ to 1 tablespoon plain whole-milk yogurt*

1. Rinse plums thoroughly. Prick skins with a fork, place in a bowl and cover. Cook at 100 percent for 4 minutes.
2. Remove cover carefully. Remove peels and pits.
3. Purée or mash fruit. Fold yogurt into fruit and serve.

Variations:
Use cottage or ricotta cheese instead of yogurt. Pour over cooked rice or mix with infant rice cereal.

BANANA AND BARLEY

Makes 1 cup

It seems to me that babies get bored with the same old grains, so try barley for a nice change of pace.

> *¼ cup quick-cooking pearl barley*
> *1¼ cups water, juice, milk or a combination*
> *½ banana, mashed*

1. In a microwave-safe dish (3- to 4-cup size), mix barley and liquid together. Cover, cook at 100 percent for 2 minutes. Then cook 10 minutes at medium setting, uncovered.
2. Add mashed banana, stir and cook, covered, for 30 seconds. Let rest 5 minutes.
3. Remove cover carefully. Taste barley for tenderness. If still too firm, cook an additional 2 minutes, covered (add more liquid if the barley appears dry).
4. Purée or serve with added liquid if needed. (Can also be served as a messy, but fun, finger food.)

CHUNKY APPLES AND SQUASH

This is a great way to serve both fruit and vegetables in one dish.

Makes ¹/₂- to 1-cup portion, depending on the size of the squash and apple used

¹/₂ small winter squash (butternut or acorn)
1 apple, peeled, cored and chopped
1 tablespoon water or apple juice

1. Slice squash in half, remove seeds, place cut side down on microwave-safe dish.
2. Cook, uncovered, at 100 percent for 5 minutes or until soft. If it is not quite cooked, continue cooking in 1-minute increments until it is tender when pierced with a knife.
3. Scrape out the squash with a spoon and place it in a 2-cup microwave-safe dish.
4. Add chopped apple and water or apple juice, stir and cover. Cook at 100 percent for 3 minutes.
5. Remove cover carefully. Stir, then allow to sit for 2 minutes, covered, to cool.
6. Mash with a fork before serving, or purée for infants. Add extra water or apple juice if it appears too dry or if you want to thin it out more.

Variation:
For older children, replace water with orange juice and add 1 tablespoon of raisins along with the apples.

SWEET POTATO PURÉE

Makes about
¾ to 1 cup

You can cook the potatoes ahead of time, but microwave them for 1 minute to warm them up before puréeing.

> *1 large sweet potato*
> *½ cup whole milk*

1. Prick potato skin. Cook at 100 percent for 7 minutes. If you do not have a carousel, turn at the 4-minute mark.
2. When done, the potato should feel hot and soft. With a hot pad hold the potato, cut it in half and scoop it out.
3. Purée with enough whole milk to make it smooth.

Variations:
Purée with yogurt or cottage cheese instead of milk.

OLD- FASHIONED MASHED POTATO

Makes a
1-cup portion,
depending on
size of potatoes

This may seem like a not-too-original recipe, but, frankly, we don't eat enough fresh potatoes. Potatoes are nutritious! This dish is rich in potassium, vitamin C and even calcium.

> *2 large potatoes*
> *¼ cup whole milk*
> *Dab of butter or margarine*

1. Prick the potatoes to let out steam while cooking. Bake at 100 percent for 10 minutes.

2. With a heat-proof mitt, remove from oven. They should feel hot and soft. Cut potatoes in half, scrape into a bowl, add milk and just a dab of butter.

3. Mash with a fork or purée. Make sure you add enough milk—babies seem to like their potatoes very wet (at least my girls do).

Variations:

Mix in a few tablespoons of cottage cheese or grated cheese. Add cooked grated vegetables of any type. Mix in a raw egg and cook an additional 3 minutes until very hot. Let rest, covered, 1 to 2 minutes. Add more milk if too dry.

CARROT CREAM

Babies like this dish because carrots are naturally sweet. This recipe tastes best if it is made with fresh, flavorful carrots, and the only way to judge flavor is to taste the carrots yourself. This dish contains milk and cheese, so serve it only if your baby has tried milk and has had no reaction.

Makes about ½ to ¾ cup

> *2 small carrots, peeled and grated*
> *1 tablespoon water*
> *1 tablespoon milk*
> *1 tablespoon ricotta or cottage cheese*

1. Mix grated carrots with the water. Cover and cook at 100 percent for 3 minutes. Let rest for 3 minutes, until carrots are very soft. (Carrots must be very tender before puréeing or they will have a grainy texture that many infants don't like.)

2. Mix in milk. Purée and add enough cheese so that the carrot mix is the consistency of thin oatmeal.

GREEN BEANS WITH RICE

*Makes about
¾ cup*

This a basic dish that you should feel free to embellish on. When your baby is old enough, add cheese or leftover cooked chopped meat. The preparation time is short, but, like all grains, rice needs time to "rest" and absorb the liquid.

> *¼ cup enriched white rice*
> *1 cup water or broth (homemade or salt-free preferred)*
> *½ cup green beans, fresh or frozen and thawed*

1. Put rice into a 4-cup bowl and add water or broth. Cover and cook at 100 percent for 3 minutes. Let rest, still covered, for 10 minutes.
2. While rice cooks, prepare the beans. If using fresh beans, trim off stems and tails. Chop beans into pieces the size of cooked rice.
3. Carefully remove cover, add green beans to rice and fluff. Add more water or broth if needed, enough to cover both rice and veggies. Cook for 2 minutes more on medium power. Let rest, covered, 3 to 5 minutes.
4. Carefully remove cover and fluff the rice. Check for doneness. Both rice and beans should be very tender. If the rice is still too firm, add another tablespoon of liquid and cook an additional 2 to 4 minutes.
5. Purée for infants; older children can eat the dish mashed with a fork and with a taste of butter or margarine added.

Variations:
Use carrots or zucchini instead of green beans. When your child is old enough to eat meat, mix in leftover pieces of finely chopped meat or poultry.

BABY BORSCHT

Parents don't usually like beets because the bright red color can make a mess out of baby's nice clothes. Many babies, on the other hand, love both the color and the sweet taste.

Makes about 2 cups

2 small fresh beets, about 2 inches in diameter
1 small carrot, chopped fine
1 to 2 tablespoons plain yogurt (optional)

1. Cut off tops and scrub beets clean. Place in a 4-cup microwave-safe bowl. Add enough water to cover the beets. Cook at 100 percent for 10 minutes, covered.
2. Remove beets from oven—they should be firm but not hard—reserve liquid. Cool beets by running them under water, then slip off skins with fingers or a knife.
3. Chop beets—they should still be a bit firm.
4. Add carrots to ¼ cup reserved liquid, cook at 100 percent for 3 minutes, covered. Let rest 2 minutes to complete cooking. Carrots should be very tender.
5. Add chopped beets to carrots and broth and cook at 100 percent for 1 minute more. Add ¼ cup of reserved beet broth if it appears dry.
6. Purée beets and carrots in a blender. Add enough reserved liquid to match your baby's swallowing ability. This can be served with a dollop of plain yogurt, or, for children who can take a few lumps, serve over leftover toast that has been cut or torn into pea-size pieces.

8

WET AND LUMPY

FOR EIGHT- TO TWELVE-MONTH-OLDS

Your little baby has left infancy behind and will be experimenting with eating with a spoon and fingers. This is a very messy time in your baby's eating development. Be prepared and don't think your child is unusual if he is uncooperative at mealtimes.

CHERRY CRUSH

*Makes about
⅓ cup*

One year when cherries were in season I developed this recipe for Sarah to try. It looks like a cherry relish, and Sarah loved it served with yogurt. Add a teaspoon of sugar before cooking if cherries are very tart.

> *10 fresh cherries*
> *1 tablespoon fresh orange juice*

1. Wash and pick over cherries, remove pits and chop into small pieces.
2. Mix with the juice in a 2-cup microwave-safe dish. Cover and cook for 2 to 3 minutes, until cherries are very tender.
3. Serve warm over cereal, yogurt, or alone. When cooled and drained, this makes a nice finger food but remember that cherries can leave juice stains.

PURÉED ROOT VEGETABLES

*Makes 1 to
1½ cups*

Feel free to vary the root vegetables you use in this recipe (see the variations below). This makes about 1 to 1½ cups, so there will be some for you to enjoy, too. This is so delicious that you can increase the portions, but you will need to cook a little longer.

> *1 carrot*
> *1 parsnip*
> *1 potato*
> *¼ cup milk*

1. Peel and chop all vegetables into uniform pieces about ½ inch in diameter (remove core of parsnip if very fibrous).

2. Cover with water in a 4-cup bowl and cook 5 minutes at 100 percent. Let rest 5 minutes. All vegetables should be tender when pierced with a fork. If the vegetables are not yet soft, cook for an additional 2 minutes.
3. Drain and purée in a blender, or beat with a mixer if making larger portions. Use just enough milk to make the vegetables smooth.

Variations:
Use any combination of these vegetables: acorn squash, hubbard squash, butternut squash, turnips, rutabagas.

ZUCCHINI AND BUTTERNUT SQUASH MIX

This dish is pretty to look at because of the contrasting colors. Better still, it is nutritious and delicious to eat.

Makes 1 to 1½ cups

> *1 small butternut squash*
> *¼ cup vegetable, beef or chicken broth (preferably without salt added)*
> *½ cup fresh zucchini, finely chopped*

1. Slice the butternut squash in half, remove seeds and quarter. Cut off peel from one quarter of the squash and chop into ½-inch pieces.
2. Put squash into a 3-cup microwave-safe bowl. Add broth. Cover and cook at 100 percent for 4 minutes. Cook longer in 1-minute increments if squash is not tender when pierced wih a fork.
3. Add zucchini to squash, mix and recover. Add more broth if needed. Cook at 100 percent for 1 minute and let rest 1 minute before serving. Zucchini should be very tender.
4. Mash or drain and serve as a finger food. Cook and eat the rest of the butternut squash yourself!

BROWN RICE WITH BLUEBERRIES

Makes ½ cup

This dish has the sweetness of a dessert, but when served with a dollop of yogurt, a glass of milk or cheese slices it has the nutrition of a main meal.

> *½ cup cooked brown rice*
> *¼ cup fresh blueberries*

1. Cook brown rice in the microwave (see page 112) or put some aside the next time you cook brown rice for yourself. Even in the microwave, brown rice still takes about double the time to cook as white rice.
2. Wash and pick over berries. Put in a dish. Cover and cook 2 minutes at 100 percent.
3. Mix in cooked brown rice. Cook 1 minute more, covered, at 100 percent.

Variations:
Instead of brown rice, try cooked white rice, cooked barley or kasha.

POACHED APRICOTS

Makes ½ cup

For a sweet but nutritious treat, try this dish on your little one.

> *1 or 2 fresh apricots*
> *½ cup any 100 percent fruit juice—pear, orange or apricot, for example*

1. Scrub fruit and slice in half. Remove pit. Place sliced sides down in a microwave-safe bowl and add juice.
2. Cook at 100 percent for 2 to 3 minutes, uncovered. Cool, remove peel if desired and mash or chop into small pieces. Serve with a spoon or drain and serve as a yummy but messy finger food.

COMPLETE DINNERS

Here are some dishes that can serve as complete meals in one bowl.

CAULIFLOWER CRUNCH

Many adults do not put cauliflower on their most favorite vegetable list, but to little people the flavor, funny shape and texture can be quite appealing. If your baby does not like this dish at ten months, try it again when he's older.

Makes 1½ to 2 cups

> 1 cup cauliflower, chopped (fresh if you can get it, or frozen and thawed)
> 1 small potato, peeled and cut into ¼-inch cubes
> ¼ cup leeks, chopped (optional)
> ¼ cup evaporated or whole milk
> 1 ounce cheese (use American, Muenster, Montery Jack or mild Cheddar),
>   chopped, sliced thin or grated

1. Place all vegetables with milk in a 4-cup microwave-safe dish. Cover and cook at 100 percent for 4 minutes. After 4 minutes, the potatoes and cauliflower should be tender when poked with a knife. If not, continue cooking in 1-minute increments until tender. Add more milk if needed.
2. When tender, mix in cheese, recover and let cheese melt.
3. Serve as is, mashed, puréed or drained and as a finger food.

TINY TOT TURKEY

··

This makes a 3-cup portion, so freeze half for another meal

This is a complete meal in one bowl. Just serve with milk and baby will be eating from all four food groups. It may taste a bit bland to you. That's because no salt is added. Remember, babies don't need added salt and have not developed an appetite for it yet.

> 1 1/2 *cups water*
> *Dab of butter*
> 1/2 *cup white rice, uncooked*
> 1 *carrot, peeled and finely chopped or grated*
> 1 *to 2 ounces ground turkey meat*

1. Heat water and butter at 100 percent for 2 minutes in a 4-cup bowl.
2. Add rice and carrots to hot water. Cook, uncovered, at 100 percent for 3 minutes. Stir and let rest 10 minutes, covered.
3. Stir and cook, uncovered, 3 minutes more at 100 percent. (Rice should be almost tender. If it looks dry, add a tablespoon of water.)
4. Add ground turkey and distribute evenly throughout rice. Cover and cook at 100 percent for 2 minutes more. Let rest, covered, 5 minutes, until cool enough to eat and to allow for complete cooking of rice.

Variations:
Add peas or chopped green beans, fresh or frozen, at the same time turkey is added. Allow an additional 1 to 2 minutes resting time to cook vegetables before serving.

CHEESY CORN PUDDING

This is a filling main dish, not a dessert. I call it pudding because that's what it looks like. Try to make it when fresh corn is available.

Makes 1½ cups

> ½ cup thawed frozen corn or the corn from 1 fresh ear
> 1 cup whole milk
> ¼ cup cornmeal
> 1 to 2 ounces cheese (use American, Monterey Jack, Muenster or mild
>   Cheddar)

1. Mix corn, milk and cornmeal together in a 4-cup bowl. Cook, covered, for 3 minutes at 100 percent. Stir after cooking. Add more milk if it appears dry. (The moisture content of cornmeal varies according to the weather and the age of the meal, and this can affect cooking times. If after the first 3 minutes of cooking it has not thickened, cook, covered, in additional 1-minute increments until it starts to thicken. Stir after each cooking period. If it is too dry and the cornmeal tastes grainy, add more milk and cook in 1-minute increments until the grains are soft and the whole mixture is the consistency of cooked oatmeal.)
2. Once the cornmeal is soft and mushy but still a little wet, fold in the cheese and let rest 2 minutes. Serve as is or roll into little balls and serve as a finger food.

Variations:
Stir in fresh chopped tomato along with the cheese. Or add grated carrots or peas right at the beginning.

BABY'S FIRST STEW

Makes 1½ cups

This is a Lilliputian version of grown-up stew, delicious and easy for little mouths to chew.

> 1 small potato, peeled and chopped into pea-size pieces
> ¼ cup green beans, chopped, fresh or thawed frozen
> 1 tablespoon water
> 1 to 2 ounces ground or finely chopped fresh lamb or beef
> ½ cup fresh tomato, chopped, or ¼ cup tomato purée or sauce (preferably
>   without salt added)

1. Mix potatoes and green beans and water in a microwave-safe bowl and cover. Sprinkle with water.
2. Cook at 100 percent for 4 minutes. Let rest 2 minutes. Potatoes should be soft.
3. Mix in lamb or beef and tomato. Cover again and cook at 100 percent for 3 minutes. Stir and let rest 3 minutes, covered.

9

THE NEXT STEP

For Ten- to Twenty-four-Month-Olds

 Here are one-dish meals without any spices. In most cases the recipes are complete meals. They usually contain three out of the four food groups. That means they will provide three of the following: a protein source, a grain, a fruit or vegetable and something from the dairy group. Serve each dish with something from the missing food group, such as a glass of milk, a piece of fruit or glass of juice, or a slice of bread, and your child will have a perfectly "balanced" meal.

Of course your child does not have to eat something from all four food groups at every meal to be well nourished. The fruit you serve at snacktime or the milk before bed all contribute good nutrition too.

EASY SPINACH SOUFFLÉ
. . . .

*Makes 1½
cups*

The microwave cooks egg mixtures so that they easily produce a nice soufflé effect. Serve with a slice of bread, toast or some cooked rice to make a complete meal.

> ½ box frozen or 8 ounces cooked spinach, well drained
> 2 ounces any mild cheese, grated or chopped
> 1 egg
> 2 tablespoons milk

1. If using frozen spinach, make sure excess liquid is squeezed out. Then beat all ingredients together vigorously.
2. Cook, uncovered, at 100 percent for 2 minutes. Stir and cook again until egg appears "dry," about 2 minutes more.

LENTIL STEW
. . . .

*Makes 1¼
cups*

Lentils may not be a regular part of your menu, but kids really like them. Serve this with a slice of good bread, a fresh chopped or sliced tomato and a glass of milk for a well-balanced meal.

> ¼ cup lentils
> 1 cup water
> ½ cup tomato juice
> 1 carrot, finely chopped (about 2 tablespoons)
> 2 tablespoons celery, chopped very fine (optional)

1. Rinse and pick over lentils. Mix lentils with water in a 4-cup dish.

2. Cook, covered, at 100 percent for 3 minutes. Stir and cook on medium setting for 5 minutes. Let rest, covered, for 10 minutes. Lentils should be soft and tender. If they are still firm, cook again for 2 minutes at 100 percent.
3. Drain off excess water and add tomato juice and finely chopped carrot and celery. Cook again for 5 minutes, covered, on medium setting. Let rest 5 minutes. Lentils and vegetables should be very soft.

Variations:
After step 3, mix in cooked pasta such as orzo or elbow noodles. Stir in while still hot and let rest for 2 to 3 minutes until noodles warm up.

Macaroni and Cheese

Macaroni and cheese has an Italian heritage, but now it is as American as apple pie. The easy way to cook macaroni is on the stove top, not in your microwave oven. Cook the noodles first, then assemble this dish for your microwave. All that is needed to make this a complete meal is a fruit or vegetable. So serve some on the side or offer tomato, carrot or fruit juice as a beverage.

Makes 1½ cups

> 1 cup cooked pasta (elbow, pastina or orzo)
> 1 tablespoon milk
> ¼ cup grated mild cheese
> ¼ cup cottage cheese

1. Mix all ingredients. Cook, uncovered, for 2 minutes at 100 percent.
2. If you have a browning unit you can gently brown the top.

Variation:
Chopped cooked vegetables can be added at step 1.

TURKEY CHOWDER

Makes 1 cup

The longer this sits, the better it tastes. Try making it a day ahead and storing it in the refrigerator. Serve it with a slice of bread or a good roll and you've got a complete meal.

> 1 potato, peeled and grated
> ½ cup broth
> 2 ounces fresh or ground turkey
> 1 tablespoon frozen peas or corn, defrosted
> ½ cup milk

1. Put potatoes in a bowl, add broth and cook, uncovered, for 3 to 4 minutes, until tender. Let sit, covered, for 1 or 2 minutes to complete cooking.
2. Add turkey to hot cooked potatoes and mix well. Add defrosted peas or corn and milk. Cook 2 minutes, uncovered, at 100 percent. Let rest, covered, 2 to 3 minutes.

BEEF AND BARLEY SOUP

Makes 2 cups

Barley is another kids' favorite. This is a very nutritious soup. Serve it with some veggies on the side or mix in leftover vegetables as suggested in the variation below and a glass of milk to make the meal truly "balanced."

> ¼ cup quick-cooking pearl barley
> 1½ cups broth (preferably unsalted)
> 1 to 2 ounces ground beef

1. Cover barley with broth and cook, uncovered, at 100 percent for 3 minutes in a 4-cup bowl. Let rest, covered, 10 minutes.
2. Stir in ground meat so it is evenly distributed.
3. Cook, uncovered, at 100 percent for 4 minutes more. Stir and let rest, covered, 10 minutes before serving.

Variations:
Mix in leftover cooked, chopped vegetables. Or stir in chopped fresh vegetables at step 2 and cook along with the meat.

CHICKEN WITH RICE

This is a favorite of Emily's. This dish contains something from every food group but dairy. Serve with a glass of milk or offer yogurt or a pudding made with milk for dessert.

Makes 2 cups

    1½ cups chicken broth
    ⅔ cup instant brown or white rice, uncooked
    1 drumstick, or the meat from ½ chicken breast, skin removed
    1 to 2 tablespoons fresh vegetables, chopped into pea-size pieces (carrots, onions,
        peas, beans, broccoli, corn)
    ½ cup chopped fresh mushrooms

1. Heat 1 cup broth for 2 minutes, uncovered, at 100 percent in a 4-cup dish. Add rice and cook, covered, for 2 minutes, then let rest 10 minutes. Rice should still be a little crunchy.
2. Chop chicken into bite-size pieces. Layer chicken in the bottom of a 4-cup microwave-safe cooking dish, place vegetables and mushrooms on top of chicken, then cover with cooked rice and add ½ cup more broth.
3. Cook at 100 percent, uncovered, for 5 minutes. Let stand, covered, for 5 minutes before serving.

SUMMER VEGETABLE STEW

Makes 3 cups

Here is a recipe for all you summer gardeners who have more veggies than you know what to do with. This makes a large portion, enough for freezing. When preparing, chop all the vegetables into pieces that are small enough for baby to eat. I like to serve this with melted cheese on toast or chopped chicken on the side for protein.

1 small new potato, chopped
1 baby carrot, chopped
¼ cup chopped zucchini
½ cup asparagus, cut into 1-inch pieces
1 tomato, preferably peeled
2 tablespoons peas, fresh or frozen and defrosted
¼ cup corn, fresh or frozen and defrosted
1 clove garlic, chopped fine
2 to 3 fresh basil leaves, chopped

1. In a 4-cup dish, cook potatoes and carrots with 1 tablespoon water, covered, at 100 percent for 3 minutes.
2. Remove from oven. Stir in remaining vegetables and garlic. Cover and cook 2 minutes at 100 percent. Stir in basil and cook 2 minutes more at 100 percent.
3. Remove from oven. Taste for doneness. If feeding a child under 12 months, I recommend cooking the vegetables until they are tender enough to be mashed with a fork. If more cooking is needed, cook in 1-minute increments until done.

PASTA, PEAS, TOMATOES AND CARROTS

When you make pasta for the rest of the family, put some aside for your little one and make this tasty dish. This recipe needs some protein to make it balanced. Serve it with chopped leftover meat or chicken or with just a dollop of cottage cheese mixed in.

Makes 1½ to 2 cups

1 small carrot, grated or chopped fine
1 fresh tomato, peeled and diced
2 tablespoons peas
1 cup cooked pasta, cut into bite-size pieces, or 1 cup cooked orzo noodles

1. Put carrots and 2 tablespoons water in a microwave-safe dish. Cook at 100 percent for 3 minutes.
2. Add fresh tomatoes and peas and cook, covered, for 3 minutes more. Carrots should be soft and tender.
3. Pour over cooked pasta.

Variation:
Serve with cottage cheese stirred in.

SCALLOP STEW

. . . .

Makes 1 cup

The beauty of scallops as a baby food is that they have no bones and require no elaborate cleaning. This is a very healthy meal. Serve with a slice of bread or mix in some rice so baby has something from the "bread" group too.

> *3 ounces scallops*
> *⅓ cup milk*
> *¼ cup diced fresh mushrooms*
> *1 ounce mild Cheddar, American, Muenster, or Monterey Jack*

1. Cut scallops into bite-size pieces if they need it. Mix scallops, milk and mushrooms together. Cook at 100 percent, covered, for 2 minutes, then stir. Scallops should feel firm when pressed—be careful, though, they will be hot.
2. Mix in cheese and let rest 3 to 5 minutes. This will allow for complete cooking and cheese will melt.

Variations:

Add cooked peas or other leftover vegetables. Or stir in cooked potatoes or noodles.

FISH CASSEROLE

. . . .

Makes 1½ cups

Using fish fillets reduces the risk of bones, but pick through the fish with clean fingers just to be sure. Serve with rice, noodles or a slice of bread for a balanced dinner.

> *½ small onion, sliced very thin*
> *1 small carrot, sliced as thin as possible into julienne strips*
> *2 ounces white fish fillet (sole, cod, pollock)*
> *3 tablespoons plain yogurt*

1. Place vegetables on the bottom of a 2-cup microwave-safe dish, add 1 tablespoon water and cook, covered, at 100 percent for 3 minutes.
2. Lay fish on top of vegetables, then spread yogurt over fish. Cook at 100 percent, uncovered, for 2 minutes. Cover and let rest 2 to 3 minutes.

BRAISED BEEF

This is really like a simple beef stew, only you can use ground beef instead of cubed beef, if you'd like. A small glass of milk and half a roll are all you need to create a totally balanced meal.

Makes 1½ to 2 cups

1 small onion, chopped fine.
3-inch piece celery, chopped fine
1 carrot, chopped fine
½ cup beef stock
Dab of butter (about ½ teaspoon)
3 ounces beef chuck, cut into ¼-inch cubes, or 3 ounces ground beef
¼ cup fresh mushrooms, chopped
¼ cup tomato sauce, tomato purée or tomato juice

1. Cook onion, celery and carrot in stock, uncovered, in a 4-cup bowl at 100 percent for 4 to 6 minutes, until vegetables are tender.
2. In a separate dish melt butter by cooking in the microwave 1 minute at 100 percent. Add meat and mushrooms; coat with butter and cook 1 minute at 100 percent.
3. Stir in tomato sauce and cooked vegetables. Cook, uncovered, at 100 percent for 2 minutes. Let stand for 5 minutes to allow beef to cook through completely and flavors to blend.

CHICKEN LASAGNA WITH WHITE SAUCE

This is a bit more time-consuming than most of my recipes, but it tastes good and makes a large portion. This is a complete meal in one dish. It contains milk, protein, vegetables and noodles.

> 3 cooked lasagna noodles or 5 no-cook microwave lasagna noodles cut into 3-
>   inch pieces, or 1 cup cooked elbow noodles
> 1 cup White Sauce (recipe opposite)
> 1 chicken breast, boned, skinned and cooked
> 2 ounces grated or chopped cheese (mild Cheddar or Muenster)
> ½ cup green vegetables (peas, chopped broccoli, diced green beans), cooked or
>   frozen and thawed

1. If using the no-cook microwave lasagna noodles, prepare them by rinsing as the box instructions state.
2. Make sauce using recipe opposite.
3. Chop cooked chicken.
4. Pour ¼ cup sauce in the bottom of a 2-cup microwave-safe dish.
5. Layer noodles to cover bottom, then top with half of the cooked chicken, half of the vegetables, and half of the cheese. Repeat this layering once more, ending with the remaining sauce on top, and sprinkle with 1 tablespoon grated cheese.
6. Cook at 100 percent for 3 minutes, then let rest 5 minutes.

WHITE SAUCE

....

2 tablespoons butter
2 tablespoons flour
1 cup milk

Makes 1 cup

1. Melt butter by cooking in the microwave 1 minute, uncovered, at 100 percent.
2. Stir flour into melted butter, add milk and mix well.
3. Cook, uncovered, at 100 percent for 3 minutes. Stir to blend evenly. It should be the consistency of sour cream. If it becomes too thick, mix in some extra milk.

SARAH'S RICE WITH
RED OR GREEN PEPPER SAUCE AND CHEESE
....

Sarah has always loved peppers, either fresh or cooked. We made up this recipe to use up some peppers and to try something different on rice. Serve it with a glass of milk and fruit for dessert.

Makes 1½ cups

2 whole peppers—red, green or yellow (red is best)
1 cup cooked rice (see page 111)
1 ounce mild Cheddar, American or Muenster

1. Wash, core and remove seeds from peppers. Slice in half. Cook, covered, for 5 minutes at 100 percent. Let rest 2 minutes.
2. Chop and purée peppers while hot in a blender or food mill.
3. Pour over cooked rice and top with a slice of yellow cheese. Cook, uncovered, in the microwave for 1 minute, just until cheese melts. Rice, vegetables and cheese can be stirred together before serving.

MINI MEAT LOAF

Makes 1 small meat loaf equal to 2 to 3 kid-size portions

This is a terrific recipe for picky vegetable eaters because vegetables are cooked right into the meat loaf. Serve with a glass of milk.

> 4 ounces ground beef or ground turkey
> ½ cup any assorted fresh vegetables, grated or chopped very fine (carrots, green beans, peas, mushrooms)
> 1 egg
> ½ cup bread crumbs or crushed cereal such as unsweetened flake cereal (corn or wheat flakes are good)
> Catsup (optional)

1. Mix all ingredients (except catsup) together with your hands until they are well combined. Add enough bread crumbs so that the loaf will hold its shape.
2. Shape into a 2-inch-thick meat loaf (decorate with a strip of catsup, if desired).
3. Cook at 100 percent, covered, for 3 minutes. Let rest for 5 minutes.

MEATBALL STEW

Makes 6 small meatballs equal to 2 to 3 kid-size portions

When Sarah and Emily's grandparents were visiting I was testing this recipe, and it was such a big hit we had to make more for the adults to enjoy. Basically, it is the above recipe for meat loaf, rolled into little balls and cooked in broth. Serve with barley, rice, noodles or even between bread as a sandwich. Offer a glass of milk to drink or yogurt for dessert.

> Mini Meat Loaf ingredients
> 1 cup beef broth

1. Take above recipe for Mini Meat Loaf and complete to step 2. Shape the mixture into 6 or 8 small uniform meatballs.
2. Heat the broth in a 4-cup dish by cooking 2 minutes at 100 percent. Add raw meatballs. Cover and cook 2 minutes at 100 percent.
3. Carefully remove cover and turn meatballs. Cook 2 minutes more at 100 percent, covered. Let rest 3 minutes before serving.

SWEET POTATO AND CARROT PIE WITHOUT THE CRUST

I call this a pie, but it has no sugar. It is made with one egg, so it is rich in protein and can be a main meal. Serve with chopped tomato and a slice of bread and you have a balanced meal. My friend Gale adds grated nutmeg when she makes this for her daughter Kara.

Makes 2 cups

> *1 sweet potato*
> *1 carrot, finely grated*
> *¼ cup plain yogurt*
> *1 egg*
> *1 tablespoon raisins (optional)*

1. Cook sweet potato at 100 percent for 5 minutes, or longer if it is very big. Prick the skin before cooking.
2. Carefully remove the meat of the potato. In a bowl, mix in the carrot and yogurt, then the egg; blend until smooth. Add the raisins if you are using them. If the mixture appears dry, add another tablespoon yogurt.
3. Cook at 100 percent, uncovered, for 2 minutes. Stir, cook 1½ minutes more. Let rest 2 to 3 minutes. This tastes best if served as soon as it cools. Serve with a dollop of cold yogurt.

COUSCOUS WITH VEGETABLES

Makes 2 cups

Serve couscous to give your child a taste of Moroccan cooking. Couscous is such a delicious food and children seem to like the texture, which is something like that of cream of wheat. Serve it with cooked chicken or chopped beef to add some protein.

> 1 teaspoon butter
> 1 cup any combination of fresh vegetables, chopped fine (green beans, peas, broccoli, carrots, asparagus, spinach)
> 1½ cups water or broth (any flavor)
> ¾ cup quick-cooking couscous

1. Heat butter 1 minute at 100 percent in a 4-cup dish. Add vegetables and toss with butter.
2. Pour in water or broth. Cook, uncovered, 2 minutes at 100 percent. Stir and cook at 100 percent power for 1 minute more. Vegetables should taste tender.
2. Stir in couscous. Cook for 1 minute at 100 percent. Let rest, covered, for 5 minutes.
3. Toss with a fork before serving. Add a tablespoon of water, milk or broth if the couscous tastes a bit dry.

Variations:
Add leftover cooked meat, tofu, even chopped hard-cooked egg.

Bulgur with Dried Fruit and Ground Meat

Bulgur is cracked wheat, a wholesome, tasty grain that is easy to cook in the microwave, but, like rice, most of the cooking is done while "resting" in hot water. This makes a good-size portion. The only food group missing here is a serving from the dairy group. Serve it with a glass of milk.

Makes 2 cups

> *1½ cups cooked bulgur (see page 79)*
> *1 teaspoon butter*
> *2 ounces ground beef, turkey, lamb or pork*
> *2 tablespoons chopped raisins, prunes or dried apricots*

1. Heat the cooked bulgur with the butter by cooking, uncovered, for 1 minute at 100 percent. Stir to blend in butter.
2. Add 1 tablespoon water and the ground meat to the cooked bulgur. Mix well and cook at 100 percent for 2 minutes, covered.
3. Add chopped fruit and cook 2 minutes at 100 percent, covered. Let rest, covered, for 2 to 3 minutes before serving. Serve with cold yogurt, cooked fruit or applesauce.

FOODS TO SHARE

The following are some baby-food ideas that can double as first-course appetizers for Mom and Dad. Follow my serving suggestions and you'll have complete meals for baby.

BEAN PURÉE

Beans are a terrific, inexpensive source of protein.

1 can chick-peas or kidney beans (my kids like kidney beans best)
1 garlic clove, minced, or 1 teaspoon powdered garlic
1 teaspoon lemon juice
1 teaspoon olive or vegetable oil

For Baby
Rinse ¼ to ½ cup beans thoroughly in water. This removes much of the sodium. Mash with a fork. Serve with cooked rice, vegetables (either some cooked carrots or chopped fresh tomato) and a cup or bottle of milk.

For Mom and Dad
Mash remaining drained beans with the garlic and other ingredients. Place in a microwave-safe dish and cook at 100 percent for 90 seconds. Stir and spread on crisp crackers.

EGGPLANT GHANOUJ
. . . .

The name of this dish is wonderful when babies try to pronounce it. It's delicious and flavorful, too, so try it and enjoy it.

> *1 whole eggplant, washed*
> *½ teaspoon cumin*
> *2 cloves garlic, minced*
> *¼ teaspoon pepper*
> *1 to 2 tablespoons olive oil*
> *1 to 2 tablespoons lemon juice*

For Baby
Bake the eggplant whole with skin pricked at 100 percent for 12 minutes. It should feel hot and soft all around. Let rest 5 minutes. Slice in half. Scrape out about ¼ cup of the meat for baby. Mash or purée for little ones or cut into cubes and toss with a little butter for older children. Serve with some cottage cheese for protein, a slice of bread and fruit slices for dessert.

For Mom and Dad
Scrape out the remaining eggplant and mash with a fork. Stir in seasonings, oil and lemon juice until well combined. Add more oil or lemon juice if it is too dry. Season with more pepper and salt if desired. Serve on crisp crackers.

AVOCADO AND TOMATO SALSA

Kids like fresh tomato and avocado unadorned. Mashed with some simple flavorings, these vegetables become a delicious appetizer for Mom and Dad.

> 1 ripe avocado
> 1 fresh tomato
> 1 tablespoon chopped onion
> 1 tablespoon lemon juice
> ¼ teaspoon Tabasco (optional)

For Baby

Chop one-quarter of the tomato and one-quarter of the avocado into bite-size pieces. Serve as a finger food or with cooked chopped egg, meat or cheese for protein and a slice of good bread.

For Mom and Dad

Mix all ingredients together, including onion and lemon. Mash until smooth, add enough hot sauce to taste and serve with nacho chips.

10

THE SOPHISTICATED EATER

FOR FOURTEEN- TO THIRTY-SIX-MONTH-OLDS

 *Here are one-dish meals with herbs and spices that taste almost like grown-up food.*

RISOTTO

Makes 1½ to 2 cups

This rice-and-vegetable casserole comes from Italy. One time I didn't have any rice on hand and substituted quick-cooking barley. The result was great, so try one and then the other. Serve with a glass of water or juice.

> 1 teaspoon butter
> 1 tablespoon chopped onion
> 1 cup broth
> ½ cup raw rice
> 1 tomato, chopped
> ½ cup chopped green beans (fresh or frozen and thawed)
> 1 ounce cheese (ricotta, cottage, Cheddar or American)

1. Heat butter in a 4-cup dish for 1 minute at 100 percent. Stir in onion. Cook 1 minute, uncovered, at 100 percent.
2. Add broth and rice. Cook at 100 percent for 5 minutes, uncovered. Let rest, covered, 10 minutes.
3. Add tomato and green beams. The rice should be wet and moist. If it looks dry, add another 2 tablespoons broth or water. Remove cover, cook at 100 percent for 3 minutes. Cover and let rest 3 minutes. If rice is not tender, cook an additional 2 to 4 minutes. Stir in cheese just before serving.

Variation:
Stir in a few tablespoons of cooked chopped meat in the final resting stage.

LENTIL PIE

This is like a meat loaf but without the meat. I adapted it from a recipe called lentil loaf   *Makes 2 cups*
that I cook regularly. Lentils combined with milk and egg make this dish rich in protein.
Serve with a glass of milk or yogurt for dessert.

> *½ cup raw lentils*
> *2 cups water*
> *1 egg*
> *¼ cup evaporated or whole milk*
> *1 tablespoon onion, grated or chopped very fine*
> *½ teaspoon dried thyme, or an equal amount of poultry seasoning*
> *½ to ¾ cup crushed cereal flakes such as Corn Flakes, Special K or Wheaties*

1. Cook lentils in water, in a 6- to 8-cup tightly covered bowl, for 5 minutes at medium power. Let rest 5 minutes. The lentils will double in volume and should be tender. Cook at medium power for another 2 to 4 minutes if they are still firm.
2. Drain lentils. Mix all remaining ingredients together with lentils. Add enough cereal flakes so that the mixture can almost hold its shape.
3. Press mixture into a lightly greased 2-cup microwave-safe dish and cook at 100 percent, uncovered, for 2 minutes. Stir and cook an additional 3 minutes. Let rest a few minutes, then turn upside down onto a plate. It should plop out in one whole piece. Cut into wedges and serve with a tomato sauce or cooked and puréed peppers.

PAELLA, SORT OF

. . . .

*Makes 1½
to 2 cups*

A real paella is more complicated than this version. All paella is delicious and very pretty to look at because it has lovely color contrasts. This is a good adaptation that toddlers like. Add the spicier ingredients marked optional to match your little one's taste preferences. Serve with a glass of milk or a milk-based pudding for dessert.

*1 teaspoon butter or margarine
½ cup rice
1 tablespoon onion, chopped fine (optional)
1 teaspoon chopped garlic (optional)
1 cup tomato juice, or ½ cup tomato sauce mixed with ½ cup water
¾ to 1 cup water
2 ounces any combination of poultry or fish (If you can, use 1 ounce of fish
    such as a fillet or scallops and 1 ounce of chicken, skinned, boned and
    chopped into small pieces so it will cook thoroughly.)
½ cup peas (fresh or frozen and defrosted)
1 jarred roasted pepper, rinsed and chopped (optional)
2 to 3 black olives, rinsed, pit removed and chopped (optional)*

1. Melt butter by cooking it at 100 percent for 1 minute in a 4-cup dish. Stir in rice, onion and garlic, if using, then cook at 100 percent for 1 minute, uncovered.
2. Add tomato juice and ¼ cup water, and cook at 100 percent for 5 minutes, uncovered. Let rest 10 minutes, covered, after cooking.
3. Fluff rice, add ½ cup water, cook, covered, 5 minutes at 100 percent.
4. Arrange fish and/or poultry in an attractive manner on top of rice, and cook, covered, 3 minutes.
5. Sprinkle with peas, roasted pepper and olives. If rice appears dry, pour in about ¼ cup water. Cook, uncovered, 2 minutes, then let rest 5 minutes, or until rice and vegetables are tender and cool enough to eat.

Fish Cakes

Fish is now recognized as being truly a health food. If it seems too bothersome to make or you think baby won't like it, give this recipe a try. You may be surprised at how simple and satisfying fish can be. This recipe is easy to freeze and then reheat. Your school-age kids will love this cooked and served like a burger. Serve with a side dish of your baby's favorite veggies and a glass of milk.

Makes 4 to 6 small fish cakes

> 8 ounces cooked or fresh white fish (cod, halibut, pollock)
> 1 large potato to yield 1 cup mashed potato
> 1 egg
> ¼ cup bread crumbs, plain or seasoned, or crushed cornflakes
> Tomato purée, red pepper purée or catsup (optional)

1. If using fresh fish, place in a microwave-safe dish, add 1 tablespoon milk, cover and cook at 100 percent for 3 minutes. Let rest in dish while potato cooks.
2. Prick potato skin with a fork, then cook about 3 to 5 minutes. It is done if it feels evenly hot and soft.
3. Flake cooked fish and carefully search for any bones.
4. Remove potato from skin into a bowl. Mash with a fork, add flaked fish and cool slightly before adding raw egg (the egg will cook into lumps if the potato is too hot). Mix with your hands until ingredients are well combined. If mixture is too wet, add a few bread crumbs; if dry, add a little bit of milk—mixture should hold its shape and not crumble.
5. Shape into 4 to 6 2-inch patties. Roll in bread crumbs or crushed cereal.
6. Cook 1 patty 2 minutes, 2 patties 3 minutes and 4 patties 7 minutes. Fish cakes should feel hot and firm to the touch when pressed. Serve with tomato purée, red pepper purée (see page 106) or catsup.

Variations:

Serve with a slice of cheese melted on top. Use rinsed, drained tuna instead of fresh fish.

BEEF STEW

· ·

Makes 3 cups

This makes a large portion and is one of those recipes that taste great on day two. Cook in a 4-cup dish. Serve with a glass of milk. If you plan to freeze, do so before adding dumpling.

> *1 teaspoon butter or margarine*
> *½ small onion, chopped (optional)*
> *1 garlic clove, chopped (optional)*
> *½ cup potato, cubed into ¼-inch pieces (skin can be left on)*
> *½ carrot, diced*
> *1 cup tomato juice*
> *½ cup water*
> *4 ounces beef chuck, cubed into ¼-inch pieces*
> *¼ cup green beans or peas (fresh or frozen and thawed)*
> *½ teaspoon cinnamon (optional)*

1. Melt butter at 100 percent for 1 minute. Add onion and garlic, if using, and cook for 1 minute at 100 percent, uncovered. Skip to step 2 if omitting garlic and onion, and don't use the butter or margarine either.
2. Add potato, carrot, tomato juice and ½ cup water to onion and garlic mixture. Cover and cook at 100 percent for 4 minutes. Let rest, covered, 2 minutes. Potato and carrot should be tender but still a little firm. Cook an additional 2 minutes if they are still very hard.
3. Add cubed beef, green beans or peas and cinnamon. Cook 3 minutes, covered.
4. Stir and cook 1 minute more. Let rest 5 minutes, then serve.

To Thicken Gravy:

If you like a thick stew, try the following: Before step 3, remove ¼ cup of the gravy. Mix with ¼ cup cold water, and stir in 2 teaspoons flour until smooth. Add to stew and continue with steps 3 and 4.

To Serve with Dumplings:

> ½ cup flour
> 1 teaspoon double-acting baking powder
> 1 egg
> 1 tablespoon milk

1. Mix together flour, baking powder, egg and milk, and stir into a thick paste. Add another tablespoon of milk if it looks too thick.
2. Drop 1 large spoonful into the hot stew at step 4. (There must be plenty of liquid in the stew in order for the dumplings to cook. Add more beef broth or tomato juice if it looks dry.)
3. Cover and cook at 100 percent for 2 minutes. Let rest, covered, about 2 to 3 minutes until dumplings are cooked and no longer wet.

Moussaka
. . . .

Makes a 2- or 2½-cup portion

The true recipe for moussaka is time-consuming and more than most mothers would want to take on for just one small portion. I love moussaka, so I developed this supereasy rendition, which is a meat-and-eggplant stew with a yummy topping. (If freezing, freeze before adding topping.) Serve with a slice of bread or a roll and water, juice or milk to drink.

> *1 cup cubed, peeled eggplant*
> *1 teaspoon butter or margarine*
> *1 tablespoon onion, grated*
> *2 ounces ground lamb or beef*
> *¼ cup stock (beef, chicken or vegetable)*
> *¼ cup tomato purée*

Topping:
> *1 egg*
> *¼ cup yogurt*
> *1 ounce grated cheese*

1. Salt eggplant and let sit.
2. Place butter or margarine in a microwave-safe dish and cook at 100 percent for 1 minute. Add onion and cook 1 minute more.
3. Rinse and pat eggplant dry. Add eggplant and lamb or beef to onion and the stock. Cook at 100 percent for 3 minutes, uncovered.
4. Add tomato purée and mix thoroughly.
5. Mix egg, yogurt and cheese together, pour over meat mixture and cook, uncovered, for 3 minutes at 100 percent. Let rest 1 to 2 minutes covered.

MILD MEXICAN LASAGNA

When cooking a Mexican dish, I discovered that in casseroles, soft tortillas take on the characteristics of noodles (soft and tender) and absorb a lot of flavor. That makes them perfect for little children. This dish contains all four food groups, so just serve with something to drink.

Makes 2 cups

> ¼ cup frozen or fresh corn
> ½ cup canned tomato purée or tomato sauce
> ½ cup canned kidney beans, rinsed
> 2 soft corn or flour tortillas (about 6 inches round)
> ½ cup cottage cheese
> 1 tablespoon mild grated cheese

1. Mix corn, tomato purée and beans together.
2. Place 1 tortilla in the bottom of a round 2-cup microwave-safe dish. Feel free to tear the tortilla into smaller pieces to fit your dish.
3. Layer half the vegetable mix, then top with cottage cheese, cover with another tortilla and repeat the layering, using all the remaining vegetable mix.
4. Cook, uncovered, at 100 percent for 3 minutes. Sprinkle on grated cheese. Cover and let rest 2 to 3 minutes.

Variation:
Use mild salsa instead of tomato sauce or purée.

DAVID'S TUNA AND RICE

Makes 1½ to 2 cups

Here is an American classic. Dress it up by adding a few nutritious vegetables and you've got a dish that satisfies your peace of mind and your toddler's appetite.

½ of a 6.5-ounce can tuna, rinsed
1 cup cooked rice (see page 111)
2 tablespoons chopped or grated American, mild Cheddar, Muenster or
*   Monterey Jack cheese*
¼ cup vegetables, your choice (peas, fresh chopped tomato, green beans)
1 tablespoon milk
1 tablespoon mild cheese to melt on top

1. Mix tuna, rice and chopped or grated cheese together so that they are distributed evenly. Arrange vegetables attractively on top of the rice and tuna mix.
2. Pour in milk, and cook at 100 percent for 3 minutes. Rice mix should be heated through. Sprinkle cheese on top, cover and let rest 1 minute until cheese melts. Serve when cooled.

Variations:
Substitute cooked noodles, millet or any other cooked grain for rice (see "My Top One Hundred" for cooking other grains).

Pork, Vegetables and Orzo

. . . .

Kids love the rice-shaped orzo noodles, so this dish is always a winner. I like it, too, because   *Makes 2 cups*
it's a nice way to serve three different vegetables: carrots, green beans and tomatoes. I
prefer it made with tomato purée because purée makes the dish juicer and smoother, but
fresh tomatoes work, too. The only food group missing is the dairy group. Serve with a glass
of milk or offer some yogurt or pudding for dessert.

> *1 small carrot, chopped fine*
> *½ cup water*
> *2 ounces fresh chopped pork*
> *1 fresh tomato, chopped, or ¼ cup tomato purée, or 1 tomato from a can*
> *¼ cup green beans, cut into ½-inch pieces*
> *1 tablespoon chopped onion*
> *1 cup cooked orzo noodles*

1. Cook carrot in water in a 4-cup bowl, uncovered, for 2 minutes at 100 percent. Carrot
   must be cut into small pieces to cook properly.
2. Mix all remaining ingredients except orzo with carrots. Cover and cook at 100 percent
   for 2 minutes. Carefully remove cover, stir and cook again, covered, for 3 minutes.
3. Remove from oven. Carrots should be tender. Let rest 2 minutes, then stir in orzo. The
   temperature of the pork mixture should quickly warm up the cold orzo noodles.

Variations:
Use cooked rice instead of orzo, beef instead of pork.

COUSCOUS WITH BEANS AND VEGETABLES

Makes 2 cups

This makes a good-size 2-cup portion, enough for two children or leftovers the next day. Serve with a glass of milk or add a slice of American cheese in the last resting stage and this dish will have a serving from every food group.

> 1 teaspoon butter or margarine
> ½ small onion, finely chopped
> ½ cup quick-cooking couscous
> ¼ cup vegetables (your choice), finely chopped
> 1 cup broth or water
> ½ cup cooked or rinsed canned beans (kidney, lima, garbanzo, etc.)

1. Melt butter by cooking it, uncovered, at 100 percent for 1 minute. Mix in onion and cook, uncovered, 1 minute more.
2. Add couscous and vegetables to onion and butter. Mix well, then add broth or water, mix again and cook, uncovered, at 100 percent for 3 minutes.
3. Sprinkle beans on top of couscous. Before cooking again, add more water or broth if the grains appear dry. Cover and cook at 100 percent for 1 minute more. Let rest 2 minutes. Vegetables and couscous should be tender.

CHICKEN CURRY

Makes 2½ cups

When Emily was about fifteen months old, my husband was serving himself a dish of leftover chicken curry in our kitchen. Standing at his side was Emily, begging for a taste, and he succumbed to her request. To my surprise, she not only wolfed down the small sample but asked for more. The recipe that follows is a modified version of what I serve at the adult table. Serve this with water or juice to drink.

½ cup cooked chicken (see page 83), chopped into small cubes
½ cup plain yogurt
5 to 10 seedless grapes (red or green), chopped
½ teaspoon curry
1 cup noodles or rice, cooked

1. Mix together chicken and yogurt, stir in fruit and cook at 100 percent for 2 minutes.
2. Stir in curry and let rest 2 minutes, covered. Serve with the noodles or rice.

Variation:
Add 1 chopped banana or 1 apple, peeled, cored and chopped or grated, in place of grapes.

VEGETABLE QUICHE WITH A TOAST CRUST

Yogurt can be used instead of milk in this recipe, which will give it an unusual and delicate taste. This nutritious dish contains a serving from every food group.   *Makes 2 cups*

¼ cup yogurt (or milk)
1 egg
1 ounce American, Cheddar, Muenster or Monterey Jack cheese
1 cup vegetables, your choice (chopped mushrooms, chopped cooked spinach,
   chopped broccoli or any combination)
1 slice toast made from good bread such as whole wheat or bran

1. Mix all ingredients except toast and blend thoroughly.
2. Press the toast into the bottom of a 2-cup microwave-safe dish. Tear it to fit.
3. Pour egg mixture over toast.
4. Cook at 100 percent, uncovered, for 2 minutes. Gently stir without disturbing the bread. Cook again at 100 percent for 2 minutes. Let rest, covered, for 2 minutes. Mixture should be firm in the center when cooked.

SHEPHERD'S PIE

Makes 3 cups

For most of us this recipe brings back memories of the school cafeteria. But it made its way onto school lunch menus because kids simply love it, and your little one will, too. It's also very nutritious: it contains protein, starch, vegetables and even some milk in the potatoes.

1 large baking potato
1 teaspoon butter or margarine
About ¼ cup milk
4 ounces ground beef
½ small tomato, or 1 tablespoon tomato purée, or 1 tablespoon catsup
1 tablespoon chopped onion (optional)
½ cup frozen corn, defrosted under tap water, or fresh corn

1. Prick the skin of the potato and cook it at 100 percent for 5 minutes or until it is hot and feels soft.
2. Carefully remove the meat from the hot potato, add butter or margarine and enough milk to mash the potato properly and set aside.
3. Mix ground beef with tomato and onion (if using). Cook, uncovered, at 100 percent for 1 minute. Stir and mash any lumps and cook 1 minute more.
4. Carefully layer corn on top of meat and cook at 100 percent for 1 minute.
5. Spread mashed-potato mixture over meat, making a crust. Cook at 100 percent, uncovered, for 2 minutes. If you have a browning unit, brown the top, or put it under the oven broiler for 2 minutes to crisp up the potatoes a little.

Variations:
Use peas instead of corn or a combination of the two. Try adding chopped mushrooms to the hamburger mix. Sprinkle grated Parmesan cheese on top for the last minute of cooking once the whole mixture is assembled. This does not have to be layered, either. Feel free to smush it all together.

FISH WITH VEGETABLES

Here is an easy and tasty way to serve fish. Cooking in olive oil and using turmeric and garlic heightens the flavor. Serve with a glass of milk and all four food groups will be included.

Makes 1½ cups

½ cup chopped green pepper
1 clove garlic, chopped fine
½ cup broccoli florets, cut into bite-size pieces
2 teaspoons olive oil
½ teaspoon turmeric
1 cup cooked rice or noodles
2 ounces fish fillet (pollock, cod, haddock, etc.), cut into chunks about ¼ inch
    in size so that you can spot any bones if they are present
1 tablespoon water

1. Mix pepper, garlic and broccoli with olive oil. Cook, uncovered, for 3 minutes at 100 percent.
2. Add turmeric, cooked rice or noodles, fresh fish and water. Cover and cook 2 minutes. Let rest, covered, until cool enough to serve—about 2 to 3 minutes.

Variation:
Leave out the rice or noodles and serve with a slice of bread or a cooked potato.

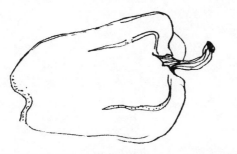

TURKEY CHILI

Makes 2 cups   Two things children love: turkey and chili. So I combined the two to make this tasty dish, which freezes nicely. Serve with a slice of bread and a glass of milk.

1 teaspoon butter or margarine
1 tablespoon onion, chopped
1 clove garlic (optional)
4 ounces ground or chopped leftover turkey
½ cup canned kidney beans, rinsed
¼ teaspoon mild chili powder
1 cup canned or fresh chopped tomatoes

1. Melt the butter or margarine by cooking it at 100 percent for 1 minute. Add onion and garlic, if using. Cook at 100 percent for 1 minute more, uncovered.
2. If using uncooked ground turkey, mix it thoroughly with onion and garlic and cook at 100 percent for 2 minutes. If using leftover turkey, add it in step 3.
3. Add beans, cooked turkey, chili powder and tomatoes. Mix well, cover and cook at 100 percent for 2 minutes. Let rest 2 minutes covered.

11

BREAKFAST FOR LITTLE CHAMPIONS

Breakfast can be the most important meal of the day, a favorite one, too, particularly on the weekend when the family schedule is not as busy as it is during the week.

The microwave oven allows you to serve your baby delicious, warm breakfasts with very little fuss. If you plan ahead, breakfast can be assembled the night before, refrigerated, then cooked in the morning while you make toast and pour some coffee for yourself.

When your baby first starts on solids, just stick with simple, unadorned cereals such as infant cereal, then progress to farina and oatmeal, which are a bit thicker.

By age ten months your child should be able to sample all the recipes in this chapter. Of course, in the recipes that call for dried or fresh fruit, make sure the fruit is chopped to a small enough size to match your baby's eating ability. Remember, too, that when serving cooked eggs they must be cooked thoroughly to kill any salmonella. That means no runny spots. And never cook an egg in the shell. It will explode, making a *very* big mess. So forget about hard-boiled eggs in the microwave; use the stove top instead.

BREAKFAST RICE

Makes 1 portion

You'll want to start this cereal the night before, because rice has a long cooking time.

½ cup rice
1 cup milk
½ to ¾ cup water
¼ fresh banana, chopped into small pieces
1 tablespoon raisins

1. The night before, mix rice, milk and ½ cup water together in a 4-cup bowl. Cook, uncovered, at 100 percent for 3 minutes. Let rest 5 minutes, covered. Stir and cook at 100 percent 2 minutes more. Remove from oven. Stir and cover. Let sit in refrigerator overnight.
2. First thing in the morning, remove rice from refrigerator, add ¼ cup water if all liquid has been absorbed and cook 2 minutes at 100 percent, covered.
3. Add bananas and raisins. Cook 2 minutes more at 100 percent. Let rest 10 minutes covered.
4. Serve with added milk or yogurt.

FARINA OR CREAM OF WHEAT WITH FRUIT COMPOTE

There's an ongoing debate about the proper name for this soothing cereal. Is it farina or cream of wheat? No matter, many children regard it as a special treat. This dish should find its way onto your table when breakfasts are more leisurely or when you want to create something a little more fun.

Makes 1 portion

> ¾ *cup water*
> 2 *tablespoons farina*

1. Heat water for 1 minute at 100 percent.
2. Add farina, cook 1 minute, stir and serve with milk, cream, sliced fruit or Fruit Compote (see page 180).

OATMEAL

In England they call it porridge; we call it oatmeal; kids everywhere enjoy it.

Makes 1 portion

> ⅓ *cup oatmeal*
> ¾ *to 1 cup water*

1. Mix oatmeal and water. Stir and cook for 1 minute at 100 percent, uncovered.
2. Stir, and cook again for 1 minute at 100 percent. Pour milk on top, add slices of banana, or serve with Fruit Compote (see page 180).

Variations:
Stir in raisins before cooking and then proceed as directed. Sprinkle on a little nutmeg or cinnamon too.

MAKE-AHEAD APRICOT OATMEAL

*Makes 1
portion*

Put this together before going to bed, then pop it into the oven just before breakfast.

⅓ cup oatmeal
¾ cup milk
1 tablespoon dried apricots, chopped very small

1. Mix all ingredients together before going to bed. Cover and place in the refrigerator.
2. Remove from refrigerator and cook, covered, at 100 percent for 2 minutes. Stir and cook 1 minute more.

Variations:
Substitute chopped raisins, dried figs or dried dates for apricots.

BAKED EGGS

*Makes 1
portion*

Eggs are a quick, convenient protein source and a perfect finger food. Make sure they are always thoroughly cooked before serving to baby.

1 egg

1. Place the egg in a custard cup and gently prick the yolk without smashing it.
2. Cook at 100 percent for 1 minute (1½ to 2 minutes for small ovens).

BAKED EGGS WITH SPINACH AND CHEESE

¼ *cup frozen chopped spinach, defrosted*
1 *egg*
1 *tablespoon grated cheese*

Makes 1
portion

1. Place the spinach in the bottom of a custard cup and top with egg. Prick yolk and cook at 100 percent for 2 minutes.
2. Sprinkle with cheese, cover and let rest 1 minute or until cheese melts. Transfer to a separate dish to prevent finger burns.

PUFFY SCRAMBLED EGGS

2 *eggs*
2 *tablespoons milk*

Makes 1
portion

1. Mix eggs and milk in a 2-cup dish.
2. Cook 1 minute, at 100 percent, uncovered, stir, then cook 1 minute more. Eggs should appear dry—no runny spots.

Variations:
Add grated cheese. Mix in chopped fresh tomato or other pieces of finely chopped cooked vegetables.

FRUIT COMPOTE

Makes 1 portion

Serve plain, with yogurt or hot cereal, or even on top of pudding. Use fruit compote to replace syrup on waffles, pancakes or French toast.

> ¼ *fresh peach, peeled*
> ¼ *fresh pear, peeled*
> 4 *slices banana*
> 2 *tablespoons apple juice*

1. Mix all ingredients and cook at 100 percent, uncovered, for 2 minutes.
2. Mash with a fork or purée.

FRUIT COMPOTE (USING CANNED FRUITS)

Makes 1 portion

> 3 *canned peach slices*
> ½ *canned pear, sliced*
> 4 *slices fresh banana*
> 1 *tablespoon juice from can*

1. Mix together with juice and cook, covered, at 100 percent for 1 minute.
2. Mash or purée.

BREAKFAST PANCAKES

You can't cook a decent pancake in the microwave, but the next time you make pancakes, make extra and freeze them.

Makes 4 pancakes

Reheat frozen pancakes by placing them on a microwave-safe dish. Cover them with Fruit Compote (see opposite), then cook at 100 percent for 1 minute. All ingredients will be warm and "fresh" tasting. Tear into pieces for your toddler or let them be eaten as a finger food. Below is a recipe that makes only 4 pancakes, just enough for the cook and one little eater.

1 cup all-purpose flour
½ teaspoon salt
2 tablespoons sugar
1 teaspoon baking powder
2 tablespoons butter
1 egg, beaten
¾ cup milk

1. Sift together the flour, salt, sugar and baking powder.
2. Melt the butter by heating it 1 minute in the microwave at 100 percent.
3. Add melted butter, egg and milk to flour mixture.
4. Cook in a greased griddle or frying pan on the stove, and then serve topped with Fruit Compote as suggested above.

12

SOMETHING SPECIAL

NUTRITIOUS SNACKS AND DESSERTS

 Snacks can be an opportunity to have fun and to introduce new foods. Most children, by the time they reach their first birthday, will actually need something to carry them from meal to meal. Here are some suggestions that have served me well. Most of them are ordinary ingredients combined in a different manner or served with something unusual.

SNACKS

MILK

- In the blender, purée milk with fresh fruit to make a fruit shake. Serve in a glass with a fresh fruit garnish on the side of the glass.
- Serve with a straw.
- Serve in a funny plastic cup.

CHEESE

- Serve cheese in small cubes or grated.
- Spread crackers with cottage cheese and fruit.
- Melt cheese on toast or bread by micro-waving 1 minute at 100 percent, and make funny faces on the cheese with chopped vegetables.

FRUIT

- Serve cubed fruit, any washed berries or sliced grapes.
- Make an apple sandwich: Core an apple, slice into rings, spread with peanut butter and eat like a sandwich (for good chewers only).
- Bake apples or poach pears (see pages 67 and 105).

VEGETABLES

- Shred or slice any vegetables.
- Serve a potato or a sweet potato cooked and cubed.
- Cook whole peas in the pod. Prick the pod with the tip of a sharp knife first, then cook for 1 to 2 minutes at 100 percent in the microwave. Cool, then let your child pick out the peas one by one.

GRAINS

- Serve cooked leftover rice or noodles, slices of good whole-grain bread or dry un-sweetened cereal. All are good, whole-some snacks.

DESSERTS

A good chocolate bar is on lots of grown-ups' lists of favorite foods, but when it comes to our kids, we must use some judgment. Most children (not unlike their parents) have a hard time showing any restraint when sweet foods are close at hand. However, if you start sweets too soon or give them too often, you may set yourself up for food battles and poor nutrition, because your child will learn to not eat unsweetened foods.

I recommend holding off on desserts until about fifteen months. Prior to this age children don't know what they're missing, and they can satisfy their natural sweet tooth on cooked or fresh fruits. Until they go to school you can control what your children eat, and since nutrition is so important to their development, you'll be trying to give them the best food you can. To me that means no candy, no added sugar or honey, and definitely no soda. Does that mean no cookies or cake are *ever* allowed? No, I just don't recommend that they be served regularly.

By age fifteen months you will have had time to lay a foundation for good eating patterns and will have established rules about when and how dessert is served. In our house dessert shows up unpredictably. It might be after a meal, as part of a party, or it could be made for a special snack. What is important is to establish that dessert is not given on demand and must not replace other nutritious foods given at mealtime.

The recipes I've selected are all low in sugar and consist of nutritious, wholesome ingredients such as milk, eggs and tasty cooked grains. Most of my desserts are sweetened with sugar. I've tried to keep the sugar low, but if you feel the need to cut back even more, you can. Reduce the amount I've recommended by half and the recipe will still work out okay. Dessert should be a source of pleasure, so have fun cooking and have even more fun when you see your little one gobbling up the good stuff you created. *Warning:* All puddings come out of the oven VERY HOT, so make sure you let them cool before serving. Try the "clean-finger poke test" (see page 4) to make sure.

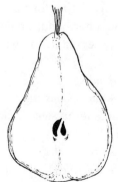

POLENTA PUDDING

Makes 2 cups

This is a very easy dessert to make, and foolproof, too.

> *½ cup cornmeal*
> *2 cups water*
> *2 to 4 tablespoons sugar (use the lesser amount if you want a subtle sweet taste)*
> *½ teaspoon vanilla*

1. Mix cornmeal, water and sugar together in a 4-cup bowl. Cook, uncovered, 5 minutes at medium power. Stir and mash lumps, cook 3 minutes longer on medium power.
2. Remove from oven, stir in vanilla and let rest 10 minutes. The pudding will continue to thicken as it cools.

CHOCOLATE BREAD PUDDING

Makes 1½ cups

There is no accounting for taste. Sarah loves every type of bread pudding I've ever made. Emily, on the other hand, prefers the rice or grain puddings and has refused bread pudding every time I've served it. I'm with Sarah on this one.

> *¾ cup milk*
> *2 to 4 tablespoons sugar (use the lesser amount if you want a subtle sweet taste)*
> *½ ounce unsweetened baking chocolate, finely chopped*
> *1 egg*
> *1 teaspoon vanilla* ·
> *1 slice stale bread or toast, torn into small pieces*

1. Mix together milk, sugar and chocolate. Cook, uncovered, at 100 percent for 2 minutes.
2. Beat egg. Stir hot chocolate mix, then mix 4 tablespoons of the chocolate into the beaten egg.
3. Pour the egg-and-chocolate mix back into the remaining chocolate and blend well. Add vanilla and bread and cook again for 2 minutes, uncovered, at 100 percent. Cover and let rest until cool enough to eat.

GRANDMA'S VANILLA PUDDING

This recipe was developed by my mother to satisfy her granddaughters' sweet tooth, while giving them lots of good nutrition, too.

Makes 1½ cups

   ¼ cup sugar
   1 tablespoon cornstarch
   1 cup milk
   1 well-beaten egg
   1 teaspoon vanilla

1. Mix well sugar, cornstarch and milk in a 4-cup bowl. Cook at 100 percent for 2½ minutes, uncovered. Stir.
2. Mix ¼ cup of the hot milk mixture into the beaten egg and combine thoroughly. Return egg-and-milk mixture to the remaining milk and cook again, uncovered, at 100 percent for 1 minute more.
3. Remove from oven and stir in vanilla. Cover and allow to cool before serving. Serve as is or with ripe fresh fruit, Fruit Compote (see page 180) or chopped canned fruit.

GRANDMA'S CUSTARD

Makes 1 to 1½ cups

This custard has a wonderful creamy taste and is very rich in protein. It can be a temporary meal replacement when regular meals are not appealing to sick little ones.

> *2 eggs*
> *½ cup milk*
> *2 tablespoons sugar*
> *¼ teaspoon vanilla*

1. Beat eggs, milk, sugar and vanilla and pour into a 2-cup dish.
2. Cook at 100 percent for 2 minutes, uncovered, stir and cook 2 minutes more. It may still be soft when you take it out of the oven, but it continues to cook and will eventually thicken.
3. Cover and let rest for 5 minutes. Refrigerate or serve warm. (Custard cooked in the microwave is lumpy. If you want it smooth, purée in the blender or food processor while still hot, then cover and cool.)

TAPIOCA

Makes 2½ cups

Tapioca is a wonderful, old-fashioned pudding. This version is easy to make because you don't have to separate the eggs and whip the whites. It's great for busy mothers, who need to keep cooking simple whenever they can!

> *1 egg*
> *2 tablespoons sugar*
> *3 tablespoons quick-cooking tapioca*
> *2 cups milk*
> *1 teaspoon vanilla*

1. Mix egg, sugar, tapioca and milk thoroughly in a 4-cup bowl. Let stand 5 minutes, then mix again before cooking.
2. Cook at 100 percent for 3 minutes, uncovered, stir and cook at medium power for 4 minutes more. Mix in vanilla, cover and allow to rest until cool.

Milk-and-Sugar–Free Tapioca:
This is a good alternative to the above recipe if you want to avoid milk or sugar: Substitute 2 cups apple juice for the milk and skip the sugar.

RICE PUDDING

Rice pudding is a traditional comfort food. Served warm with a dollop of yogurt or a scoop of vanilla ice cream, it's a terrific treat.

Makes 1½ cups

> ⅔ cup instant brown or white rice
> 1 cup plus 2 tablespoons milk
> 2 to 3 tablespoons raisins, chopped (optional)
> 1 egg
> 1 tablespoon sugar
> 1 teaspoon vanilla

1. Mix rice and 1 cup milk in a 4-cup bowl. Cover and cook at 100 percent for 2 minutes. Stir and cook at medium power for 3 minutes.
2. Mix together raisins, egg, sugar and 2 tablespoons milk. Then add to partially cooked rice. Cook 2 minutes more, uncovered, at 100 percent.
3. Stir in vanilla, then let rest, covered, for 10 minutes.

BREAD PUDDING

*Makes 1½
to 2 cups*

This is a good way to use up any pieces of stale bread or, better yet, leftover toast. In our house we make toast every morning, but on some days there's a slice or two left. That's the day bread pudding appears on the menu.

> 1 slice toast or stale bread
> 2 tablespoons sugar
> 1 cup milk
> 1 egg
> ½ teaspoon vanilla

1. Tear bread into bite-size pieces. Mix sugar, milk and egg together, add bread pieces and stir. Cook at 100 percent, uncovered, for 3 minutes.
2. Stir in vanilla and let cool. Cover and let rest 3 minutes.

Variations:
Add ripe bananas or peeled and chopped very ripe peaches in step 1. Add raisins in step 2.

EASY PUMPKIN PUDDING

Makes ¾ cup

This is so easy it's almost a crime.

> ½ cup canned pumpkin
> ¼ cup vanilla yogurt

1. Mix canned pumpkin with yogurt. Blend evenly.
2. Warm for 1 minute at 100 percent, covered. Stir before serving.

INDIAN PUDDING

This is a wonderful pudding if you love the taste of molasses. This recipe makes a large enough portion to feed several kids or one child and two adults.

Makes 3 to 4 cups

> *½ cup cornmeal*
> *½ teaspoon ginger*
> *¼ teaspoon cinnamon*
> *1 tablespoon sugar*
> *2 cups milk*
> *⅓ cup molasses*
> *1 egg*
> *2 tablespoons raisins (optional)*

1. Mix together cornmeal, ginger, cinnamon and sugar in a 4-cup bowl. Blend well. Add milk and molasses to cornmeal mixture and mix thoroughly. Cook, uncovered, at 100 percent for 3 minutes. Stir and cook 1 minute more. Cornmeal should be partially thickened. Break up lumps with a spoon and stir until smooth.
2. Beat egg, add ¼ cup of the hot cornmeal mixture into the egg and blend well. Pour the egg mixture back into the hot cornmeal, stirring constantly. Cook 2 minutes at 100 percent, uncovered.
3. Remove from oven, stir, add raisins, if using, and let rest 5 minutes. Serve with ice cream or cold milk.

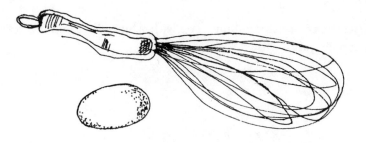

SWEET PIES FOR YOUR SWEETIE PIE

*Makes enough
to line a 2-cup
dish, or 1 pie.*

These pies are not the labor-intensive delicacies you remember from Thanksgiving. These are fast, easy, yummy and meant to be fun food for special times. Infants won't really care about them, but children fifteen months and older will. Toddlers begin to understand that dessert is quite different from what is on the rest of the menu.

Pressed Pie Crust

*½ cup flour
1 tablespoon vegetable oil
½ teaspoon baking powder
1 teaspoon sugar
1 to 2 tablespoons water*

1. Mix all ingredients with your fingers until they form a ball (this is a wonderful job for an eighteen-month-old), then knead it in the palm of your hand.
2. Press the dough into a 2-cup round dish. Feel free to tear it to fit the shape. This will not be a beautiful crust, but it doesn't take long to make and it tastes great. Cook at 100 percent for 2 minutes. Cooking continues for a minute or so even out of the oven. The crust will shrink from the sides of the bowl, so don't be surprised.
3. Fill with any of the following fillings: Grandma's Vanilla Pudding (see page 187), Easy Pumpkin Pudding (see page 190), Blackened Banana (see page 193).

Variations:
Slice fruit into the pie crust before filling. Top with whipped cream for a real treat. Serve with a birthday candle, just for the fun of it.

FRUIT TART

When your baby is a little older and interested, you'll discover that this is a recipe beginning cooks can make by themselves (with your help, of course).

Makes 2 small tarts

> *Pressed Pie Crust (see above) or a ready-made dough*
> *Cooked fruit (see "My Top One Hundred") or ready-made jam*
> *Cinnamon (optional)*

1. Using the Pressed Pie Crust or a ready-made dough, cut it into 2 3-inch squares.
2. Place a dab of cooked fruit or jam in the center of the squares. Possible fillings include cooked apples, peaches, blueberries, strawberries, or cranberries.
3. Fold each square in half on the diagonal and bake at 100 percent for 2 minutes. Sprinkle with cinnamon, if you like.
4. The filling can get very hot. Allow to cool before serving.

BLACKENED BANANA

This is an easy but different way to prepare bananas. Cooking them seems to intensify their flavor.

> *1 banana, peel on*
> *Plain yogurt or vanilla ice cream*

1. Prick the skin of the banana with the tip of a knife.
2. Cook the banana at 75 percent until the skin turns black, about 3 minutes.
3. Remove the hot, soft banana from the skin. Squish it into a bowl and top it with plain yogurt or a dab of vanilla ice cream.

COOKIE FRUIT PUDDING

Makes 1½ cups

Fast, fun and yummy. The proportions don't have to be exact on this, but you do have to have enough fruit and juice or milk to soften the cookies.

> ½ *to 1 cup crisp cookies, crumbled (graham crackers, ginger snaps, vanilla wafers)*
> *1 cup fresh chopped, peeled and seeded fruit (bananas, peaches, pears, apricots), or 1 cup canned fruit (no sugar added), chopped*
> ¼ *cup juice (any flavor) or ¼ cup whole milk*

1. In a 2-cup bowl, sprinkle one-third of the cookie crumbs and top with one-third of the fruit. Then repeat the layers of cookies and fruit twice more. When assembled, pour juice over top.
2. Cover and cook at 100 percent for 4 minutes if using raw fruit (2 minutes if canned fruit was used).

BAKED APPLES

Cheery baked apples are a fun food for toddlers who are good scoopers with a spoon.

> *1 apple*
> ½ *teaspoon lemon juice*
> *Cinnamon for sprinkling (optional)*
> *Yogurt or ice cream (optional)*

1. Wash and core apple.
2. Sprinkle with a little lemon and cinnamon, if you like, and cook, uncovered, for 3 minutes at 100 percent.
3. Serve as is or top with yogurt or ice cream.

13

ON-THE-GO FOODS

WHAT TO PACK WHEN BABY WON'T BE HOME FOR DINNER

No matter what your life-style, there will be times when your baby or child is not eating her meals at home. Babies and parents travel these days, and children eat food on subways, meals at day care, suppers in classrooms, picnics in parks and snacks in strollers; cars become temporary dining rooms. It doesn't really matter where your baby eats, but what he eats is important. The environment must be clean and stress-free; it shouldn't be so noisy that baby is constantly distracted. Also, he should not have to struggle to keep other toddlers away from his food. I feel strongly that mealtime is an opportunity for sharing and learning. The ideal situation probably is a sit-down meal with all family members in attendance, ready to share food and conversation.

But unfortunately, we can't always have that, although it's still important to duplicate the basic elements of that tradition.

A good mealtime should:

1. provide good food;
2. allow for good interaction between caregiver and child;
3. be free of interruptions;
4. be supervised to prevent choking and to encourage eating;
5. be served in a clean environment.

Will your child be traumatized if he has to eat in a car while his brothers play a loud game of License Plate? No, probably not, so don't worry about the occasional irregular and imperfect mealtime. But if more often than not your little one is eating in a poor environment, it may affect his entire attitude about what food and meals should be. So try to do the best you can to set up a healthy eating routine as often as you can.

FOODS WRAPPED BY MOTHER NATURE THAT TRAVEL WELL

ripe avocado
ripe banana
hard-cooked egg

all firm fruit with a peel—
  papaya, orange, tangerine
cucumber
tomato (firm)

WHAT TO BRING WHEN YOU WON'T BE HOME AT MEALTIME

FORMULA

Just like milk, formula will spoil if it's not kept refrigerated. Once opened or prepared, it should be used immediately, or within twenty-four hours if kept refrigerated.

Solutions:

- Buy small bottles of ready-to-use formula. They're more expensive, but they don't need refrigeration until after they're opened, which makes them ideal for car or plane trips.
- Carry cold formula or milk in a good thermos, where it will not change temperature for several hours.
- Use powdered formula and put only the powder in a bottle. Add tap water just before feeding it to baby.
- If you're staying at a hotel, ask about the availability of a portable refrigerator.

MEALS

Serving a balanced meal while traveling can be tricky, but not impossible.

Solutions:

If you are traveling to someplace that has a microwave—a friend's house or day care—send foods with baby that can be reheated in the microwave. For example, freeze and bring any of the one-dish recipes included here. Or bring a sweet potato, cook it in the microwave and ask your host for some cheese or yogurt to serve it with.

ROAD FOOD

When you're traveling, put foods into empty yogurt containers or any sealable plastic container. Egg-shaped plastic containers that stockings come in are a fun way to wrap food, too. The small boxes of cereal that come six or twelve to the pack can make easy-to-carry snacks.

Recently the American Academy of Pediatrics issued a warning against feeding a child riding in a car seat. The problem is that if the child starts to choke, the driver may not be able to get to her in time to administer first aid. So while you're in the car, entertain with toys instead of food. Toddlers can be entertained for a whole car trip if they are given several paper bags filled with toys or small stuffed animals. Don't ever use a plastic bag as a toy, even if you're there, because of the risk of suffocation.

For drinks, keep a jug of water in the car and a supply of juices in containers that do not need refrigeration. These can be transferred to a bottle or a sippy cup, or, if your little one can manage it, served with the straw.

RESTAURANTS

I will admit without any guilt that when traveling I frequent fast-food restaurants for the simple reason that they have drive-up windows. If you make smart choices, you can provide your toddler with a meal that will not be much higher in calories than one he ate at home. In general, however, the sodium content is greater in all fast foods than in the homemade versions.

Feeding your toddler a healthy meal at a fast-food spot:

- Select juice or milk to drink.
- Choose the simple items, such as a plain hamburger.
- Chicken or fish sandwiches are fried and are not a better choice than the burgers.
- French fries are high in fat, but kids do love them, so if you want to serve them, just keep the amount to a minimum.
- Ice cream or cookies at a fast-food establishment have the same nutritional value as those you'd buy elsewhere.
- For breakfast, English muffins or toast are good choices, as are eggs. Pancakes are good too; just hold back on the syrup.

Avoid foods with lots of added cheese and high-fat meats such as sausage and bacon. There is no reason to teach your kids to like these, since so many people have to give up such high-fat meats as adults.

Eating out at a restaurant with very young children can be stressful. When they are under three months you can never be sure when they'll wake up and start to fuss. At eight to ten months they've started to crawl and pull on things, and everything looks like a potential toy. By their first birthday, walking may be the new challenge, and restaurant corridors can be enticing. At fifteen months they know what "no" and "sit down" mean, but their attention span is short and pleasant dinner conversation is not high on their list of fun things to do. Once your child's second birthday rolls around you may be able to cajole your toddler into staying at the table with games and drawing, but that leaves little time for you to eat or participate in conversation. I can happily report, however, that by your child's third birthday, eating out with the whole family can once again be fun.

Don't be persuaded by well-meaning friends or your in-laws from out of town to take baby to a fine dining establishment. You'll only be a nervous wreck thinking that your baby will cause a disruption. Instead, choose a restaurant that's set up for children, or hire a sitter and enjoy the evening in peace.

Don't let me dissuade you from attempting restaurant meals. One couple I know loves to eat out, and they do so frequently with their two-year-old daughter in tow. As a result, their little girl has learned how to behave while at a restaurant, and her mom and dad report having a good time, too.

If you are going to eat out, plan ahead and consider the following suggestions for keeping baby happy:

- Check to make sure the restaurant has high chairs.
- Entertain your little one with a bowl of chipped ice.
- Ask for a package of crackers right away to keep baby occupied until food comes.
- Grilled cheese, baked potato or chopped fresh tomato are often popular with kids.
- Order a chowder or soup and spoon out the meat and vegetables for baby.
- For very young children, carry a garlic press in your purse and use it to mince what Mom and Dad have ordered.
- Tell the waitress you want to order quickly.

Traveling is our way of life these days, whether it's just to shop or to go to the office or to go out of town on business or pleasure. Because you have a child doesn't mean you should change all your old traveling activities. What it does mean is that if you are bringing your baby or toddler, you must be prepared.

14

BUGS AND TUMMY ACHES

WHAT TO COOK WHEN YOUR CHILD GETS SICK

It will happen. Overnight your busy baby will come down with a bug that will turn him into a listless, unhappy little trouper. Sometimes it's scary if symptoms are severe. Other times it's just a source of mild concern. No matter how sick your baby or toddler is, you'll want to do the most you can to keep or make him comfortable.

Despite the claims made about chicken soup, food won't cure a cold. If your child has the flu or a cold, it just has to run its course. But food can help relieve a child's symptoms and can actually be important in preventing more serious complications.

On the following pages are general feeding guidelines for when a cold, flu or fever hits your little one. This is not medical advice. If your child is sick, call the pediatrician. He can give you specific recommendations to match your baby's age and medical history.

COLDS

Here's the bad news: You can expect a young child to get several colds each year. The good news is that a cold can help your baby develop a healthy immune system that eventually will make her less susceptible to illness in the future. The golden rule when battling a cold is to offer fluids. Water, fruit juice, even defizzed soda (not diet) are all good. A child with a poor appetite should be allowed to break from the usual routine. For instance: Jell-O, a fruit shake (see page 184) or applesauce for breakfast may be more appealing than a bowl of cereal.

If you've taken your toddler off the bottle, it may be comforting and an easy way to push fluids if you give liquids in a bottle again. Once the cold is over, tell him he doesn't need the bottle anymore because he is no longer sick.

DIARRHEA

Diarrhea can range from just bothersome to serious. A baby who is having frequent loose bowel movements can run the risk of dehydration, a potentially life-threatening condition. Your goal, when diarrhea occurs, is to make sure your child is taking fluids. Clear liquids are the treatment of choice (see list below). These are foods that you can literally see through, such as apple juice and Jello-O. When fighting diarrhea, you are not striving for a balanced diet but instead are giving the baby easy-to-digest calories that won't cause any additional stress to the bowel. The BRAT diet (bananas, rice, apples and toast) may also be helpful.

The Boston Children's Hospital offers these guidelines for making sure a sick child gets enough fluids: give an infant two ounces of fluid every hour, and give a toddler four ounces of fluid every hour.

If the diarrhea persists, do not keep your baby on a clear-liquid diet for more than twenty-four hours without consulting your doctor. Your pediatrician will want to know how many bowel movements the baby has had, if there is an elevated temperature, and if vomiting is present. In most cases the pediatrician will give you the information so that you can manage at home, but that will depend on the seriousness of the condition and how long it has existed.

An infant less than six months old who is exclusively being fed breast milk or formula should not be switched to clear liquids without the advice of the pediatrician. The doctor *may* recommend diluted formula or diluting breast milk in a bottle, but always seek medical guidance before doing this. Illness is not a time to cut back on calories, which is what happens when you dilute the milk feeding. Keep in mind that in the early months of life all your baby's stools are very soft and may look like diarrhea, and breast-fed babies often have softer stools than formula-fed infants.

Be aware, however, that too much fruit juice may in itself be a cause of diarrhea. Pediatricians at Connecticut Hartford Hospital have had good results in treating unexplained cases of diarrhea. First they eliminated apple juice in the diets of five children, and the diarrhea stopped in all the children. In another group of toddlers all fruit juice was stopped, and almost half of this group were relieved of their diarrhea. Apparently, apple and pear juice may cause some unexplained continuous diarrhea. All of these juices naturally contain a sweet alcohol called sorbitol, which some people just cannot tolerate large amounts of. If diarrhea plagues your little one, try eliminating all juice for forty-eight hours. If it helps the symptoms, resume the juice but control the amounts. For example, give just one vitamin C–rich juice—about four ounces—then water.

CONSTIPATION

A baby who strains, cries or passes blood when having a bowel movement may be constipated. When constipation occurs, stools will be hard and dry. This is not usually a serious problem, but lack of fiber may be a cause and giving more fiber the cure.

Children, like adults, need healthy amounts of fiber in their diets. However, if your health-care provider recommends increasing the amount of fiber your child is eating, do it by giving your child more fruits, vegetables and whole grains. *Don't* use fiber supplements unless your pediatrician advises it. Use a whole-grain cereal for breakfast and whole-wheat toast. Also, make sure your baby is getting enough fluids. Give young children water after meals and allow them to drink it freely. And don't forget Mother

FIBER-RICH FOODS

baked beans	broccoli	potatoes
green and wax beans	carrots	prunes
bran (see page 76)	cereal, whole-grain	raisins
bread, whole-grain	corn (after 8 months)	spinach

Nature's standby: prune juice. As always, if the constipation persists, consult your pediatrician.

Too much iron can also cause constipation. Iron is not a problem when it occurs naturally in food, but iron-fortified cereal, supplements and fortified foods may be a cause. Iron-fortified formulas by themselves have not been found to cause more constipation than non-iron-fortified formulas. If you suspect you are giving your child too much iron in the form of fortified cereal, formula and vitamins combined, discuss it with your doctor. Don't switch her off iron-fortified formula casually, as it is what the AAP has found to be best for babies.

FEVER

A fever means that the child's immune system is working, and that is a good sign. During a fever the body is working hard to fight off an infection, and a baby needs extra energy because his body has a greater demand for calories. Unfortunately, as many mothers and fathers know, a fever can also bring a loss of appetite. Once again you want to offer plenty of high-calorie liquids and include light foods, but don't push them. Plan ahead and know how to take a temperature, and have the equipment ready at hand to do the job.

SORE THROATS AND COUGHS

Warm liquids seem to be particularly soothing to baby. Plain broths or even warmed apple juice can help a raw cough. Serve them in a bottle or a cup, or even with a spoon if your toddler will drink that way. For a baby who is eighteen months old or older, drinking from a straw can make taking liquids a lot more fun.

VOMITING

Immediately following a vomiting episode hold back all food and drink. You want the stomach to rest before giving it anything new to digest. Then offer only clear liquids in small amounts of two to four ounces. If your child keeps down the clear liquids, you can progress to "full" liquids (see page 204) and then on to simple solid foods. (Try the BRAT diet: banana, rice, apples and toast.) If the vomiting starts again, go back to square one. If your child can't keep down liquids, try offering a damp cloth to suck on.

As with serious diarrhea, vomiting can put your child at risk of becoming dehydrated. When your child can't hold down even clear liquids, vomits four times in two hours, has abdominal pain or blood in his vomit, it is time to call the doctor. If vomiting is occurring in combination with diarrhea and fever, get on the phone pronto. The combination of all three conditions increases the risk of dehydration.

Spitting up, or regurgitation of small amounts of food, particularly right after meals, is extremely common in infants under six months of age. Don't confuse this with vomiting, when the entire stomach contents are expelled. If spitting up is a constant problem, you might be able to curtail it by handling baby gently after feedings and laying the child on her right side for a nap after eating. In a baby less than six months of age, keep her head upright after feedings. Let the milk or food "settle" before carrying or playing.

COLIC

If I had a food remedy for colic, mothers all over the world would thank me—but I don't. Colic rarely occurs in infants older than three months, and because of this age limitation, when foods are not recommended as part of an infant's diet anyway, they can't be seen as part of the cure. No one knows for sure exactly what colic is or what causes it. The medical profession seems to agree uniformly that it is the newly working intestinal system causing spasms of abdominal cramping that result in unrelenting bouts of crying.

CLEAR LIQUIDS

These are foods that are made mostly of water and carbohydrate. A diet of clear liquids can be used only for short periods because it is inadequate in all nutrients and calories, too.

clear broth	gelatin (not diet)	carbonated soda
bouillon	water ice	(defizzed and
cranberry juice	Popsicles	not diet)
apple juice	clear, weak tea	clear fruit drinks
grape juice		

Parents describe colic almost identically. The attack comes on suddenly, and the crying is loud and continuous, persisting for several hours. The child's face can become flushed and red, the legs are drawn up to her tummy and her hands are clenched.

As suddenly as the symptoms start, they can also stop. The crying may stop either because baby is exhausted and falls asleep or because baby has a bowel movement, burps or passes gas. Late afternoon and early evening are the most common crying times. There is no "cure" for colic. Holding a baby upright or laying a warm, not hot, water bottle on her tummy may help. In some cases mild sedatives may be prescribed, so if symptoms are really severe and you're at your wits' end, talk it over with your doctor.

There is always the risk that your baby has something more serious than colic. For peace of mind, ask your pediatrician.

COMFORT TIPS

Food is not the only nourishment you'll want to provide during illness. If your child has had the good fortune to get sick at a time when you can stay home with him, then take the time to be with him. Let the housework and laundry slide. Have some nice quiet time together. Cuddle and read stories. Cook up some yummy puddings, or Jell-O if all he can have is clear liquids. If he's battling a cold, use a warm, wet facecloth to wipe his nose—it causes less irritation than tissue. A good friend of mine applies Desitin to the nose and says it works wonders.

A stuffed-up nose is very difficult for a baby who is still breast-feeding or drinks from a bottle. It is hard enough to breathe with a stuffy nose, but for a thirsty baby, a cold can be very frustrating. Infants breathe only through the nose, so use a bulb syringe to suction out the nose, and keep the head elevated. (For very small babies, buy an ear, not a nose, syringe. A small baby's nostrils are too small for the tip of the nose syringe.) Put a pillow under the baby's mattress to keep his head up higher. And get a humidifier going or sit in the bathroom with the shower running.

WHAT TO DO WHEN YOU HAVE TO WORK

Every working mother hates to leave her baby in day care or with the sitter when her little one is sick. Unfortunately, though, babies get sick, and they rarely do it on our day off. The dilemma we all have to face

---

FULL LIQUID DIET

This diet can be used as a transition from clear liquids to solids. But it, too, can be deficient and should be used only temporarily.

formula, milk or breast milk

clear broth or strained milk-based soups

puréed meat, fish, poultry or egg blended into broth or soup (8 months and older)

puréed vegetables or potatoes blended with liquid

all fruit juices

all cooked cereals

ice cream, sherbet, puddings, custards, gelatin (see pages 186–192) to find recipes for puddings that make nice treats that are good for baby, too) sometime is: Should I go to work or should I stay home and be with my child? There is no one simple answer. I have read that what many mothers do is to use their own sick days when baby is ill and then struggle to work on those days when they themselves are sick. By doing this they don't overuse their allotted number of days off. Sound familiar?

Most of us parents think that we are indispensable, and we are in the long run. In the short run, however, we can be substituted by other care givers, if they are competent and caring. On sick days, ask yourself if your child will get what he or she needs in your absence. For instance, if he needs rest, will he get it if you are not with him? Will he get the food or medicine he needs? Will he be given the special attention a sick child deserves? If the answer to these questions is yes, then it is probably okay for you to go to work.

When you must leave your child with another care giver, send along foods you know your child will like, and include his favorite toy or blanket for comfort. Make sure the care giver knows your baby isn't feeling up to par and deserves extra attention today.

THE BRAT DIET

An acronym for bananas, rice, apples and toast. This diet is a welcome solution for mothers whose babies don't want much food. The diet is considered to be bland enough for illness and contains binding fruits that will help with diarrhea.

mashed ripe bananas
rice cereal, cooked rice
applesauce, apple juice,
    cooked apples—usually
    without peel

toast (preferably white
    bread), saltines or other
    plain crackers

To take some of the monotony out of the regime, I've come up with the following variations:

rice puffs with apple juice
white rice cooked in apple
    juice

white rice cooked in
    bouillon
cooked rice mashed with
    bananas
toast spread with mashed
    bananas

15

QUESTIONS AND ANSWERS

The following questions are real problems that both friends and clients have asked me about. There is still a lot of misinformation out there about how and what to feed your baby. Some of the advice offered by friends and family may be worthwhile, but other information you get may be way off base. If you are worried about any aspect of your child's health or feeding regime, always ask your own pediatrician for specific recommendations. If you feel you would like to talk to someone about your baby's menu, I'd suggest you contact a registered dietitian. Just look in the yellow pages under "Nutritionist" or "Dietitian" or ask your doctor for a referral.

A close friend whose children are now in high school tells me I should feed my two-month-old daughter cereal so she'll sleep through the night. Will this help?

Well-meaning friends often tell parents to feed cereal in an effort to help babies sleep through the night. If only it were that simple. Several studies conducted on children do not support this recommendation, and my own experience confirms this. Our first child, Sarah, was not a good sleeper. Even after she was on solids, including cereal, fruits, vegetables, protein and grains, we still couldn't count on her to sleep through the night.

Most parents don't realize that breast milk and formula are liquid food and contain more fat and protein than cereal does. It is fat and protein that lead to a baby feeling full. So, though new parents are frequently told to start cereal before age four months, there just doesn't seem to be any hard evidence to support this advice.

I recently talked to a friend who bragged that her three-month-old baby was already on solids. Is there any harm in starting sooner than four months?

Parents often feel a sense of accomplishment when they can report that their baby is eating solid foods way ahead of other infants,

just as they do when their kids do other things ahead of schedule later in life. Until five or six months of age a baby can't communicate his or her interest or lack of it in food. A baby fed too soon isn't eating, but instead is being force-fed. Besides preventing a force-feeding situation, there may be some good medical reasons to hold off on the introduction of solids. When foods are given too soon, it can increase a baby's chances of developing food allergies and may contribute to obesity (see Chapter 4 for more information on preventing specific allergies and obesity). While the jury is still out on the obesity issue, it's safe and smart to tell parents to hold off on foods. Until four months, baby just doesn't need them. Formula or breast milk is all baby needs until then.

My mother told me that I'm starving her grandson by giving him just breast milk. He's three months old and always seems to cry at night. Could he be hungry? She says she fed me cereal when I was two weeks old.

The recommendations new parents may receive about feeding from grandparents need to be scrutinized. That advice is as old as you are. In the past twenty to thirty years, pediatricians have conducted numerous studies on when to start feeding children.

While at one time parents fed their babies solids very early in life, that is no longer advised. Breast milk and formula provide all the calories and nutrition a very young baby needs.

It is very common for babies to cry uncontrollably in the early evening. Breast-fed babies in particular can appear to be hungry because they start to feed, then abruptly stop, as if in frustration. Many child-rearing experts seem to think that at this early age children cry as a means to unwind and that it frequently has nothing to do with food. In some situations some breast-fed babies may need to be fed sooner than formula-fed babies, but this is not usually the case. If your son is growing adequately and your pediatrician says he is fine, then don't worry!

Here is a tip for handling well-meaning friends and relatives: Listen to their advice. Thank them. Tell them you will ask the baby's pediatrician. Then you can say it's the pediatrician who tells you not to feed the baby yet, and this way they can find fault with the doctor, not you.

My breast milk appears too thin. Is it possible that my milk isn't good enough to feed my baby?

New parents, and particularly breast-feeding mothers, express concern that the milk appears too thin to support their baby. They fear baby isn't getting enough. But Mother Nature designed the perfect balance of protein, fats and nutrients in breast milk. The major pharmaceutical companies who make formula have done their absolute best to copy this recipe. Formula and breast milk provide ample calories and nutrition for your baby. If you are worried that baby is not getting enough to eat, simply check with the pediatrician. Most doctors recommend weight checks at two weeks, two months and four months. Routine doctor visits will uncover any health problems.

I cook my ten-month-old a great dinner, then he eats only half of it. What's wrong?

A very common concern among parents is getting their children to eat what they think is enough. Most of us are accustomed to eating adult-size portions. For example, a parent may serve her ten-month-old a half-cup of potatoes, expecting her to finish it all because "it really wasn't much." Baby, however, eats only one or two teaspoons and quickly calls it a day. Mom and Dad become frustrated and concerned that baby isn't eating enough. Those bite-size portions may not look like much to you, but to baby they are just right. Next time, feed your baby smaller portions and refill the dish if she wants it.

My baby deliberately won't eat what I prepare, but then wants to eat ten minutes after I clean the table. Only now he wants just fruit or peanut butter.

When my daughter Sarah was about eighteen months old we had a similar problem. We came up with this solution: In the kitchen we set up a small table with a chair that was just her height. She could use this spot for playing, but I used it for food, too. If she didn't eat all her lunch, I'd put it on the table for her to pick on. This way I knew that if she was really hungry she had something to eat. It was important to me that I didn't start the habit of feeding her special-order meals. Of course the leftover food must be appetizing. You can't expect a child to eat something that is dried-out and stale-looking. A good rule of thumb is to ask yourself: Would I eat it?

Whatever you do, try not to get into food struggles with your kids. Babies will eat if they are hungry—it is just that simple. Your job is to provide your child with good, nourishing food in a pleasant environment. It is then your child's responsibility to eat. As every parent knows, or will soon learn, you can't force a child to eat if he or she does not want to—so don't bother trying. Trust your child to know what he needs. If he is hungry, he will eat. That does not mean you need to become a fast-food cook, however.

Prior to my baby's first birthday she was eating everything. Now, at fourteen months, she seems to have turned into a picky eater. I'm worried that she is not getting enough nutrition.

This is a very typical problem. The reason is simple. In the first year of life your baby tripled her weight. To do this she needed more calories per pound than a teenager requires. That rapid growth slows at age twelve months, and so does appetite. Don't panic and don't be frustrated. This decline in the amount she eats is to be expected. Keep offering small portions and allow her to eat what she likes.

My six-month-old baby appears to be very fat and I'm worried that this might become a lifelong problem.

Most pediatricians agree that how fat a baby is in the first six months of life is more a reflection of the maternal diet while pregnant than what the baby is eating now. Simply put, mothers who gain more weight are more likely to have fatter babies. This does not appear to reflect their propensity toward obesity later in life. In fact, in the first two years of life a baby's degree of fatness or even height in comparison to other children does not seem to be a predictor of how she will compare to others later in life.

Do not put a child under two years of age on a weight-loss diet. If you are concerned about your toddler's weight, get him involved in active play. Most pediatricians recommend increased exercise and less TV for weight loss. And, of course, make sensible food choices, too.

How will I know if I'm feeding a balanced diet?

Simply follow the food-group guides listed earlier and offer variety. For instance, don't always serve carrots. Mix it up. Try sweet potatoes, peas, beets and spinach, and alternate between lamb, turkey, fish and other protein foods. Serve a variety of grains such as oatmeal, rice, barley and fortified noodles. Consult "My Top One Hundred" for more ideas and easy instructions on how to prepare new foods for your child. There are hundreds of wonderful foods to prepare—introduce your child to new foods and you'll enjoy them, too.

How will I know my child is eating enough?

This is easy. The scale is the best measurement, and it is an excellent indicator. Babies and toddlers will be weighed at each

---

TO MY READERS

While writing this book I listened carefully to every concern I heard from new parents, but I am sure there are problems I have missed. If you have concerns or questions that you feel should be part of this book, I would like to hear them. If you have suggestions for menu ideas or travel tips, I'd like to learn about them, too. In short, any and all comments are welcome.

Write to me, Eileen Behan, c/o:
Villard Books
201 East 50th Street
New York, N.Y. 10022

---

doctor's visit. If there is no weight gain or an inadequate one, your pediatrician will alert you. You do not need to weigh your child between visits.

Last week I made a pudding with artificial sweetener. Without thinking I gave it to my sixteen-month-old. Is this safe to do?

Artificial sweeteners such as Equal, saccharin or sorbitol have no place in your baby's diet. First of all, a baby needs the calories in real food. Second, there is still a cloud of suspicion hanging over the safety of some of these sweeteners. Don't give them to your child. It is extremely unlikely, however, that giving your child one serving of the pudding you described will do any harm, so don't worry.

In the supermarket, sometimes I buy the marked-down meat. Is this safe to feed my baby?

Yes. Fresh cuts of meat are usually marked down at the meat counter if they are about to reach "sell by" date. These meats are still nutritious and safe to use, providing you cook them right away or immediately freeze them for later use.

How many calories does my baby need?

An "average" baby from birth to three years needs from 650 to 1,300 calories per day. Active children may need more and quiet babies less. Don't get hung up on calories. Look at your baby's behavior and general well-being. A child who is happy and energetic is sure to be eating well, so don't just focus on diet but look at the whole picture.

APPENDIX:
RESOURCES FOR PARENTS

As a new parent I could never read enough about babies, parenting and health issues. The following are resources that I myself have used and found helpful. I've listed the topics I referred to earlier in the book alphabetically. Recommended books and newsletters can be found at the end.

ALLERGIES

For more information on allergies contact:
Asthma and Allergy Foundation of America
Suite T 900
1835 K Street, N.W.
Washington, DC 20006
(202) 293-2950

BREAST-FEEDING

The Complete Book of Breast-feeding, by Marvin S. Eiger, M.D., and Sally Wendkos Olds. New York: Workman Publishing, 1987.

This book was recently revised and offers terrific information on just about every problem or concern you might have about breast-feeding.

La Leche League
La Leche League International
P.O. Box 1209
Franklin Park, IL 60131-8209
(312) 455-7730
A volunteer organization of mothers that offers support and advice to breast-feeding mothers. You can contact the parent organization in Illinois, which will direct you to a local member who can offer lots of personal support. The organization also publishes a catalog that includes breast-feeding booklets and products you might want.

Breast-feeding Your Baby, by Sheila Kitzinger. New York: Alfred A. Knopf, 1989.
Lots of pictures and very easy to read. This is a book that will confirm your decision to breast-feed.

CHILD SAFETY

"Safe Kids Are No Accident: How to Protect Your Child from Injury"
Available free by writing to:
FSI
P.O. Box 4779
Monticello, MN 55365
This is a pamphlet on child safety available from the National Safe Kids Campaign.

FLUORIDE

If you want to learn more about fluoride, write to:
American Dental Association
211 East Chicago Avenue
Chicago, IL 60611
(312) 440-2500

MICROWAVE OVEN SAFETY

According to the International Microwave Power Institute, an industry service organization in Clifton, Virginia, the best and first place to go with your concerns about your oven is the oven manufacturer. If you are having trouble with the door or hinge or you think the oven just isn't working right, look in your service manual or contact the folks you bought it from. You can also contact your state health department or the nearest Food and Drug Administration office (these can usually be located in the white pages of your state's capital city).

USDA Hot Line
(1-800) 535-4555
As the name suggests, this is a hotline operated by the USDA to answer all your questions about cooking meat and poultry. That includes questions about microwave cooking, too.

MILK-FREE COOKING

Here are some resources that can provide some basic recipes and information. If you or your child must be on a milk-free diet, I would strongly advise you to contact a registered dietitian for some individualized nutrition instruction. (Look in the yellow pages or contact the American Dietetic Association address below.)

"Good Eating for the Milk-Sensitive Person"
Ross Laboratories
Columbus, OH 43216
Recipes for cooking without milk. Free.

Lactaid
Sugarlo Company
Atlantic City, NJ 08404

Lactaid is a product that is very useful to people who can't digest the milk sugar lactose. If you have trouble locating it, contact the company listed above. They make Lactaid milk and cheese products that are carried in most supermarkets.

"Soyalac: Information and Recipes"
Loma Linda Foods
Medical Product Division
Riverside, CA 92505
Recipes for cooking without milk. Free.

NUTRITION

For a free nutrition newsletter and other health information geared toward preventing cancer, contact:
American Institute of Cancer Research (AICR)
P.O. Box 76216
Washington, DC 20013
This organization provides information about children as well as adults and older Americans, too.

American Dietetic Association
430 North Michigan Avenue
Chicago, IL 60611
This is the professional organization for registered dietitians. It publishes nutrition materials on many subjects, and if you want to locate a registered dietitian in your area but can't find one, try contacting the association at the address above.

PESTICIDES

For Our Kids' Sake,
published by Mothers and Others for Pesticide Limits
A project of:
Natural Resources Defense Council
40 West 20th Street
New York, NY 10011
This book offers suggestions for how to protect your child against pesticides in food as well as where to find pesticide-free food. The NRDC is a nonprofit organization dedicated to protecting natural resources and improving the quality of the environment. It was the NRDC and the campaign launched by Mothers and Others that led to the elimination of Alar on apples.

For more information about the Alar-and-apple scare of 1989, read:
Consumer Reports, May 1989

VEGETARIAN NUTRITION

For a free twenty-four-page booklet about planning a vegetarian diet for your child called "Teddy Bears and Bean Sprouts," call 1-800-4-GERBER.

Diet for a Small Planet, by Frances Moore Lappé. New York: Ballantine Books, 1971. This book is looked upon as the "bible" for planning a vegetarian diet. It will tell you all you need to know about combining foods to get the right balance of nutrients, specifically protein. Also includes some good recipes.

"Vegetarian Nutrition"
National Dairy Council
Rosemont, IL 60018-4233
This is a four-page brochure that does a good job of summing up the vegetarian basics. No recipes, but it is free.

WATER

Call the Environmental Protection Agency (1-800-426-4791) for a list of certified water testers in your area.

For the free pamphlet "Lead in Your Drinking Water," write:
EPA
Public Information Center
Washington, DC 20460

For information about water-filter systems, write:
National Sanitation Foundation
Ann Arbor, MI 48106

MONTHLY PUBLICATIONS

The following are the newsletters I subscribe to. All of them are good.

Nutrition Action Health Letter
Center for Science in the Public Interest
1875 Connecticut Ave. N.W., Suite 300
Washington, DC 20009-5728
The CSPI can best be described as the "Ralph Nader" of the food industry. Besides lobbying for healthier food legislation, the group publishes *Nutrition Action Health Letter*. The newsletter provides timely information on food issues, labeling, food products and even healthy recipes. It deals with children's issues as well as adult and senior citizen concerns. $19.95 for 12 issues.

Also available from CSPI is *Creative Food Experiences for Children*, a book for parents of children age three to ten to help instill a healthy awareness about nutrition and good food. $5.95.

The University of California, Berkeley, Wellness Letter
P.O. Box 10922
Des Moines, IA 50340
This publication does an excellent job of explaining health issues that concern both children and adults. Many of its articles are about food and nutrition, but the newsletter also addresses medical issues from prescription drugs to sprained ankles. $18.00 for 12 issues.

Tufts University Diet and Nutrition Letter
P.O. Box 10948
Des Moines, IA 50940
I have a special affection for this newsletter because for several years I wrote for it and learned a lot about accurately researching complex food stories. This publication deals specifically with nutrition and diet and occasionally publishes recipes. $18.00 for 12 issues.

The Growing Child,
published by Dunn and Hargitt, Inc.
22N Second Street
Lafayette, IN 47902
This is a great publication for new parents. When you subscribe you will be asked your child's birth date, and then each month a newsletter will be sent that corresponds to your child's age, beginning as young as one

month. The Growing Child does a great job of explaining the developmental stages. It does talk about feeding, but not the specifics. It offers good suggestions for age-appropriate play activities that I found very useful. $19.95 for 12 issues.

EXCELLENT NUTRITION AND FAMILY HEALTH BOOKS TO HAVE IN YOUR LIBRARY

Jane Brody's Nutrition Book: A Lifetime Guide to Good Eating for Better Health and Weight Control, by Jane Brody. New York: W. W. Norton & Co., Inc., 1985.
This book is now a few years old, but it is still the best resource I know for accurately and clearly explaining what can be the complicated world of nutrition. If you have nutrition questions, this book will help you with the answers. It includes nutrition issues from birth to old age.

The New Child Health Encyclopedia: The Complete Guide for Parents, Boston Children's Hospital. New York: Dell Publishing Company, 1987.
An excellent, easy-to-read resource. Subjects are listed alphabetically. Medical prob-

lems include a description, suggestions for prevention and customary treatment.

Child of Mine: Feeding with Love & Good Sense, by Ellyn Satter, R.D. Menlo Park, CA: Bull Publishing Co., 1986.
A very good book that offers advice on coping with eating and feeding problems in young children as well as good basic information on healthy eating principles. Not a recipe book.

Microwave Gourmet, by Barbara Kafka. New York: William Morrow & Company, Inc., 1987.
If you want to learn more about cooking for the rest of the family, graduate to this book. Easy to use, with recipes for cooking good, healthy food.

Your Baby and Child, rev. ed., by Penelope Leach. New York: Alfred A. Knopf, 1989.
An excellent resource on caring for your child from birth to the preschool years. Sleeping, toilet training, and learning milestones are all expertly addressed.

Babyhood, by Penelope Leach. New York: Alfred A. Knopf, 1976.
A book for parents with children up to age two. It will answer all your questions about physical and emotional development.

Infants and Mothers: Differences in Development, rev. ed., by T. Berry Brazelton. New York: Delacorte Press, 1983.
A month-by-month guide for the first year of life with a look at what parents can expect from their average, quiet or active baby.

The First Three Years of Life, by Burton L. White. Englewood Cliffs, N.J.: Prentice-Hall, Inc., 1985.
This book deals with the problems parents often find themselves concerned with such as: letting a baby "cry it out," crib toys, coping with older siblings, encouraging interest in the outside world. The author divides the first three years of life into seven phases. In each phase, the parent can learn what to expect from the child in terms of behavior and development, and ways to foster a healthy relationship with your child. I found the book very helpful, though I disagree with the doctor's advice about the ideal sibling spacing being three years apart.

Dr. Spock's Baby and Child Care, rev. ed., by Dr. Benjamin M. Spock and Michael B. Rothenberg. New York: E. P. Dutton, 1985.
Recently revised. A real bible for parents: First aid, toilet training and diaper changing are just a few of the concerns that are explained clearly.

INDEX

ABOUT THE AUTHOR

Eileen Behan is a member of the American Dietetic Association, a registered dietician and a mother of two. She holds a degree in home economics from Rivier College in Nashua, New Hampshire, and completed a traineeship in nutrition at Brigham Women's Hospital in Boston. She has worked for the Harvard School of Public Health and the Veterans Administration, and for five years her show "Food For Talk" aired on Boston public radio. She currently works as a nutrition consultant helping families to improve health through diet. An avid cook and the owner of four microwave ovens, she lives with—and feeds—her family in New Hampshire.